Thai Tales

World Folklore Series

Heather McNeil, Series Editor

Thai Tales

Folktales of Thailand

Retold by
Supaporn Vathanaprida

Edited by
Margaret Read MacDonald

Illustrations by
Boonsong Rohitasuke

1994
Libraries Unlimited, Inc.
Englewood, Colorado

LIBRARIES UNLIMITED, INC.
P.O. Box 6633
Englewood, CO 80155-6633
1-800-237-6124

Project Editor: Kevin W. Perizzolo
Copy Editor: Tama J. Serfoss
Proofreader: Eileen Bartlett
Interior Design and Type Selection: Judy Gay Matthews

Library of Congress Cataloging-in-Publication Data

Vathanaprida, Supaporn.
    Thai tales : folktales of Thailand / retold by Supaporn
  Vathanaprida ; edited by Margaret Read MacDonald ; illustrations by
  Boonsong Rohitasuke.
    xviii, 153 p. 19x26 cm. -- (World folklore series)
    ISBN 1-56308-096-6
    1. Tales--Thailand. 2. Tales--Thailand--Translations into
  English. 3. Tales, Buddhist--Thailand--Translations into English.
  4. Legends--Thailand--Translations into English. I. MacDonald,
  Margaret Read, 1940-   . II. Rohitasuke, Boonsong. III. Title.
  IV. Series.
  GR312.V38   1994
  398.2'09593--dc20   94-4287
                                                            CIP

To my Great-Grandmother who, night after night, entertained me with the wonderful stories that helped remind me of who I am, and why I am the way I am.

To all the Buddhist monks who keep some of these stories alive by retelling them at many Thai ceremonies.

Table of Contents

Chapter 5—*Nithan Son Khati Tam*: Tales to Make You Think *(continued)*

Chapter 6—*Tamnan*: Local Legends

Chapter 7—*Nithan Songkhruang*: Elaborate Tales

Chapter 8—*Thep Niyai*: Tales of Helpful Gods and Spirits

Chapter 9—The Place of Buddhism in Thai Life

Preface

In this book you will find 28 Thai folktales. The tales were remembered or translated and retold by Supaporn Vathanaprida. Thai folklore is rich with magical tales, humorous tales, tall tales, poetic epics, and moral tales told by Buddhist monks. Choosing the few for this book was difficult. We decided to include some of the lengthy Thai magical tales and several humorous tales. However, we were especially eager to present our reader with a good selection of the Thai monk's tales, those brief but pointed stories used to illustrate the many aspects of Buddhist thought.

If you would like to learn more about Buddhist teachings see Su's chapter at the book's end on "The Place of Buddhism in Thai Life." To learn about sources for these stories or to think about variations of these tales in other cultures, see the Notes on Tale Sources. For more good books to read see "More Books to Read About Thailand."

I hope you enjoy this book and learn from it. I have certainly learned a thing or two myself from these stories.

Margaret Read MacDonald

Acknowledgments

I want to thank the many Thai storytellers and educators whose ideas I had the liberty of adapting to confirm my beliefs and to refresh my memories. I especially thank Mr. Yut Detkhamron, whose books are a valuable resource, and from which I selected some stories to retell in English.

We express our appreciation to the following people for allowing us the use of the photographs in the design of this book.

Cover 1: Supaporn Vathanaprida
Cover 2: Alan Swensson
Ph.1: Jim MacDonald
Ph.2: Alan Swensson
Ph.3: Alan Swensson
Ph.4: Alan Swensson
Ph.5: Alan Swensson
Ph.6: Jim MacDonald
Ph.7: Alan Swensson
Ph.8: Jim MacDonald
Ph.9: Jim MacDonald
Ph.10: Vathanaprida family member
Ph.11: Chare Vathanaprida
Ph.12: Alan Swensson
Ph.13: Chare Vathanaprida
Ph.14: Supaporn Vathanaprida
Ph.15: Supaporn Vathanaprida
Ph.16: Supaporn Vathanaprida
Author/editor photo: Bev Waugh, King County Library System

Designs and illustrations were provided by Boonsong Rohitasuke.

An Honorable Member of the Association of Siamese Architects, Boonsong Rohitasuke has studied and worked in Thailand, England, and the United States. He has been a Professor in the Faculty of Architecture at Chulalongkorn University in Bangkok, and most recently worked in Seattle as an architect for the Four Seasons Hotels.

Introduction

Supaporn Vathanaprida grew up in the city of Lampang in Northern Thailand. Su heard many of the stories presented in this book as a child. Her schoolbooks were full of wonderful Thai folktales, the monks related stories whenever they spoke, and best of all Su's great-grandmother used to tell her stories each night. Su realizes now that her great-grandmother was not just entertaining her little great-granddaughter with these stories—she was *teaching* her. Teaching her the *Thai way*—the way a person should behave.

Now Su would like to pass these stories on to you. Maybe they will give you some hints about how a person should behave too.

Su is well qualified to tell these stories because she grew up in a rural area of Thailand, where the life she saw going on around her was much like that of these old folktales. She has seen woodcutters climbing their trees like Lung Ta, she has seen beautiful young ladies like the Muang Laplae maidens walk by carrying their swinging baskets of vegetables, and she has seen elephants being trained like the giant elephant in "Good Boy," because Lampang has a special training school for working elephants.

Su hopes these stories will give you a glimpse of the magical, marvelous world of Thai folklore and she hopes their messages will bestow on you a Thai "cool heart."

Great-Grandmother's Stories

Listening to Great-Grandmother's Tales

Some of the happiest moments in my life were the times I lay in my bed listening to my Great-Grandmother's stories. Every night she would come and lie in bed beside me. First, she would teach me a prayer—a very short one, which I said while she said a very long one. I had to wait patiently while she was praying. Once finished, she would tell me stories—wonderful, magical stories. Thinking back, I realize that many of these stories influenced my way of thinking, forming my habits and behavior. Many times, they consoled me when I was sad, disappointed, or unhappy. When I felt as if I was number one, I would remind myself of the story, "He Who Thinks He Is First Is Unwise," or "Who Is Best?" These stories helped me learn to become more humble, more open-minded, and more ready to learn from others. When I wanted to tell a lie, I would stop and think about "Muang Laplae" and what happened to the young man who lied in the story. If I felt injustice, I would think about "If It Belongs to Us, It Will Come to Us," then my mind would be at peace. I would no longer feel frustrated, restless, or angry. The same values helped me when I learned that my father died while I was on the plane flying home to see him. I was very sad, but I did not lose my composure. I kept thinking that sooner or later, everyone must die, and nobody can escape death, just like the stories "Medicine to Revive the Dead" and "When Death Comes." The thought helped me understand and accept the inevitable. These and many other tales that I heard a long time ago, somehow soothe me, make me happy, or at least help me be at peace with the world and with myself.

Teaching Tales of the Monks

Many of the tales my Great-Grandmother told me are stories she heard from the monks, monks' tales and *Jataka* tales. Every week, on the Buddhist Sabbath Day, my Great-Grandmother would spend one night at the *wat*, the monastery. We children had the duty of accompanying her to help carry her sleeping mat, pillow, and her basket of betel nuts.

At the *wat*, the day was spent listening to the monks as they chanted the story of Buddha's many lives and recited moral tales. People enjoyed this storytelling. I myself would come and go from the *wat* all day long. If I did not hear the whole story then, I would hear the rest of those stories from my Great-Grandmother later.

Monks' tales were composed by monks and scholars to teach some moral principle based on Buddhist teachings. Many are fables or animal tales. *Jataka* tales are stories about the lives of Buddha. But in Thailand, many other moral stories have become associated with the morals from the *Jataka* tales, and these also are known as *Chadok* or *Jataka*.

Humorous Tales with a Message

Some of the stories my Great-Grandmother told were just cunning, humorous tales like "Sri Thanonchai." These tales were satirical, and helped the commoner vent frustrations toward the elders, bosses, or rulers who were not acting as expected. They reminded those who were in high positions to be watchful and to correct their improper acts.

The Thai people, in general, do not like confrontation or conflict. Therefore, while they may not say exactly what bothers them, they *would* hint at it through a story. This desire to keep harmony is rooted in Buddhist teaching about avoiding the extremes, remaining impartial or non-involved, respecting others, showing compassion and kindness toward others, and accepting others as they are.

Nithan and Local Legends

Many of the tales my Great-Grandmother told me are *nithan* or *niyai*—fairy tales. These fairy tales have been told from generation to generation to entertain, to teach, or to keep records of certain events.

Thailand is a nation of folk and fairy tales. There are stories about almost everything—towns, caves, rivers, stars, lightning and thunder, animals, and, of course, people. Perhaps because the country is such a very old nation without written records until around A.D. 282, the Thai people had to rely on the stories told by older generations to the younger ones for the preservation of their heritage. Many of those early stories were told in verse, a device that made them easier to recall, and which fixed their form and content as they were passed down.

The Thai people originated in Yunnan in the south of China about 4,500 years ago. Chinese from the north started migrating southward around A.D. 10. By 1238, the Thai had established their kingdom of Sukhothai in the region they now occupy in Southeast Asia. As they moved south, the Thai absorbed stories from the native peoples they conquered and from other peoples they encountered such as the Mon, Khmer, and Lao. The Thai still tell stories derived from Chinese folklore. There are stories of the giant serpent Nakha, or Naga, and the Hindu gods: Vishnu, Indra, and Brahman. Other stories suggest cultural exchange with the Khmer people, who had lived in Southeast Asia before the Thai arrived. The Khmer had already adopted both Hinduism and Buddhism from India before the Thai came into contact with them. Animism was practiced side-by-side with these other beliefs.

In short, the Thai stories have many origins. Some are clearly Buddhist in origin, like the *Jataka* tales of "The Deer Buddha" or "The Two Rice Birds"; others are Indian, such as "Songkran: A Thai New Year Story"; still others, like "Twin Stars," are derived from Chinese folklore.

Local legends, too, are popular in Thailand. Temples, caves, islands, each locale has its own folktale. In this collection, "Muang Laplae" and "Mouse Island and Cat Island" are examples of tales told about specific places in Thailand. Origin tales also are popular in Thai lore. Two appear in this collection: "Why the Bear Has a Short Tail" and "The Elephants and the Bees."

An Oral Tradition to Share

As you see, the Thai tell tales of many kinds. Some Thai tales are fabricated histories and legends, others have moral meanings. Some are philosophical, while others are humorous in intent. No matter how the stories originate, one thing is certain—all these tales were meant to be told orally. These stories have a message, and those who listen carefully will find it. Passed from generation to generation, these stories last because they have universal appeal. It is true that these tales also encompass some traditions and beliefs of the Thai that are unique, and different from western ideas, but the universal appeal is still there. After all, human beings are not really very different when we look beneath the outer shells. In this book, transliterations of difficult Thai words are found in parentheses.

Chapter 1

Nithan Gohok: Lying Tales

Lung Ta, the Calm Woodcutter

In Thailand, elders are addressed as Uncle, "*Lung*" (Loong) and Aunt, "*Pa*" (Pä), or as Grandfather, "*Ta*" (Tä) and Grandmother, "*Yai*" (Yäi), if they are very old.

As he climbed, the woodcutter would have been wearing a *pakhama* (päk-a-mä), a long piece of cloth wrapped around his hip into which he could tuck his axe and his climbing sticks. The tea leaves he carried are *miang* (mi-ang), *Camellia sinensis*, considered a treat to chew on.

Lung Ta was the best woodcutter around. Whenever an unusually large tree needed felling, people always called on Lung Ta. Nothing ever unnerved Lung Ta. No matter how tall the tree, or how big its bore, Lung Ta was always undaunted. Lung Ta could do the job.

One day, some villagers began preparations to build a new *wihan* (wihän), a temple for worship. They found the chosen site crowded by a huge tree. No matter how much money the committee offered, none of the local woodcutters would attempt to fell such a tall tree. After much discussion, the committee decided that only Lung Ta could possibly cut such a tree. They contacted Lung Ta, and he agreed to cut their tree.

When Lung Ta arrived, he examined the tree with some alarm. This was the biggest, the tallest tree Lung Ta had ever seen. Lung Ta decided the best thing to do was to relax for a while, so Lung Ta sat down for a long smoke. Next Lung Ta stuffed *miang* in his mouth and thoughtfully chewed his *miang* leaves. At last, he fastened his axe and the climbing sticks around his waist, along with a bag containing his *miang* leaves, betel nuts, tobacco, and matches.

Lung Ta began slowly to climb the tree, using his climbing sticks. Lung Ta's wife, Pa Kaeo (Pä Kaeo), had followed to watch his feat. She and the villagers watched in alarm as he slowly made his way up this enormous tree. Lung Ta climbed up and up. People craned their necks until they ached, watching Lung Ta climb higher and higher. Pa Kaeo would not take her eyes off her fearless husband. A friend had to massage poor Pa Kaeo's neck as she peered up without rest.

Lung Ta climbed and climbed, until he was almost lost to sight. At last he reached the top of the tree. Taking out his axe, Lung Ta slowly began chopping away at its branches. One by one they fell, until only one branch remained. Suddenly, a storm arose. A harsh wind blew against that last branch and whipped it loose. It brushed against Lung Ta as it fell, knocking him and his possessions from the tree.

The villagers at the bottom of the tree, screamed with shock as Lung Ta, his axe, his climbing sticks, his bag, and his betel nuts, *miang* leaves, tobacco, and matches flew every which way. "Whirr ... whirr ... whirr...." The sound of their fall through the air could be heard above.

Pa Kaeo fainted at the sight of her poor husband falling through the air. Massaging her and holding perfume under her nose, her friends revived her. She opened her eyes. "How is Lung Ta?" Her friends looked up. "He hasn't reached the ground yet. Listen."

The "whirr ... whirr ... whirr..." of his falling could still be heard.

Pa Kaeo raised her head to look. At that moment Lung Ta hit the ground with a "thud." The noise of his landing was so loud that it scared the water buffalo grazing nearby. The panicked cows ran straight for the river and landed with such a splash that the entire village was soaked with the water.

As soon as they had regained their composure, the villagers rushed to Lung Ta. They could not believe their eyes. Lung Ta reclined on his side with his eyes closed. A lit cigarette dangled from his mouth as he slowly exhaled through his nose. Beside him lay his climbing sticks, neatly secured in their bag. And in his kit, his betel nuts, *miang* leaves, tobacco, and matches lay tidily in order. Around his waist, his axe hung neatly in place.

Lung Ta slowly opened his eyes. With a half smile he spoke, as if to himself. "This may be my last woodcutting job. I am getting old and slow. I barely was able to gather my axe, sticks, nuts, leaves, tobacco, and matches before I reached the ground. I am not as agile as I used to be. In my youth, I would have been able to finish weaving a basket or two while I fell, as well."

The Liars Compete

Tall tales are popular in Thailand. The legends even tell of a Liar's Pavilion, where the best liars are said to have gone to compete in their tale-telling.

In the past, every town and city would have a storyteller known as the town's best tale-spinner. This person would be well-known and respected by the townspeople. Wherever he went, people would greet him and ask for a story. It was a source of great pride to a storyteller to be able to spin the tallest tale ever. The one thing that every storyteller feared was finding someone who told better tales than he. Storytellers were always searching for new stories to tell, and they would travel far to challenge other storytellers.

This storyteller's house, like most Thai houses, was built on stilts with an empty space beneath it.

One day, an out-of-town storyteller arrived to challenge the city's most reknowned teller. He asked directions to the storyteller's home, and arrived late in the afternoon. The storyteller was taking a nap in the house, but his young son was sitting beneath the house, playing. Seeing a stranger passing, the son asked, "Dear Old Man, where are you going?" The out-of-town storyteller thought to have some fun with this child. "I am looking for my lost buffalo," he said. "Have you seen it? And is your father at home?"

The boy looked the old man over. "Yes, my father is at home. But he is taking a nap right now. What color is your buffalo? I saw several buffalo pass by a few minutes ago. Perhaps one was yours."

The out-of-town storyteller laughed delightedly, and said, "My buffalo is easy to recognize. If you had seen it, you would remember."

"Does it have something special about it, then?" asked the boy.

"I'd say so. My buffalo has long horns. In fact, its horns are so long that they almost touch the sky? Did you see it?"

Without pausing, the boy nodded solemnly and pointed a finger in one direction. "Why yes, Dear Old Man, I did see such a buffalo. It walked under my house not long ago. It went in that direction."

Hearing the boy answer in such a straight-faced manner, the out-of-town storyteller's face turned pale. If this small son of the town storyteller could tell such an outrageous lie, surely the father must tell even better stories. Try as he might, the visitor knew he could not come up with a story to best such a teller. Better to return home and prepare himself more before taking on this family of tellers. The out-of-town storyteller turned and left town quickly.

This happened a very long time ago. I, who tell this story, have not heard whether or not that out-of-town storyteller ever returned to make his challenge. If any of you have heard about this, please let me know.

The Marvelous Canning Factory

When factories were first built in rural Thailand, the local people heard reports of the assembly lines with amazement. The notion of the components of a product being carried down a conveyer belt, worked on by a line of assemblers, and emerging complete at the other end sounded like a tall tale. Soon a *real* assembly line tall tale was being passed around.

Have you ever heard of the world's most advanced canning factory? It was built recently near here. Such a canning factory has never been seen before. Fresh food is dumped into one end of the machine, and that machine will wash, clean, chop, separate, and can the food—all by itself!

People have been coming from far and wide to see this marvelous canning factory. They just shake their heads in bewilderment when they see it in action. I haven't seen the machine yet, myself, but each person who goes to see it comes back with the most fabulous canning factory story heard yet.

One person told me, "These machines were so advanced. The workers fed raw bananas into them, still on the stalk. In just minutes, the bananas came out the other end completely processed. There were dried bananas, deep-fried bananas, barbecued bananas, and sugar-coated bananas. All from that one bunch of raw bananas. I tried some of them. They were all delicious!"

The next visitor saw even more wonders. "What you saw was fascinating, but not as wonderful as the things I saw. When I toured the factory, they were feeding the machines live, pregnant pigs. Within minutes, these pigs came out as five-starred pork soup and barbecued pork. The unborn piglets came out as crispy, barbecued pork on sticks with garlic. The pork fat was all separated and put into containers, and the skin and bones were turned into fertilizer, packaged in equally weighted sacks."

Nithan Gohok: **Lying Tales**

But a third visitor had an even more fabulous story to tell. "The day that I toured the factory, we arrived as it was getting dark late in the afternoon. They were herding cows into the machines to make canned meat for the army. The manager was busy with guests and could not attend to the machines.

"After the manager finished with his guests, he came to the machines and tasted the canned meat. It was too bland. Someone had forgotten to push the buttons for salt and fish sauce. The manager stopped the work right away. 'Put all of this canned food back into the machines,' he said. 'We must add in the salt and fish sauce.' Then he looked at his watch. 'It is too late to reprocess all of this today. We will wait until tomorrow to can it again.'

"So the workers put all of the canned meat back into the machine. They pushed the reverse button on the machine, and the machines began to run again. Only this time, they worked backwards. Into the back end of the machine went the canned meat. Out the front end of the machine backed the whole cows. All of those cows walked back out to their pasture, where they continued to graze until the next day.

"The bit of canned meat which the manager had tasted had come from the left flank of a young heifer. That heifer grazed away in the field, wondering how it happened that she suddenly had a small hole on her left flank."

Well that must have been a remarkable canning factory. Perhaps you visited it and have a story to tell yourself?

The Liars Contest of the King

The teller of this incredible tale might well have been a winner at the Thai Liar's Pavilion! The *baht* (bät) mentioned in this story are Thai money.

There once was a selfish king who always did just as he pleased, regardless of the consequences to others. If his actions brought hardships to other people, he gave this no thought at all.

Now, above all else, this king loved storytelling. He wanted to have storytellers performing in his palace every day. Every storyteller in the land had been summoned to the palace at one time or another. In fact, everyone in the land who knew any story at all had been brought before the king to entertain him. At last there came a day when no new story was left in the land. The king had heard them all!

Still, the king wanted to hear *more*. He decided to announce a contest. Anyone who could tell a tale so tall that even his four court counselors had to admit it was a lie would receive a reward. This lucky man would receive a lump of gold as large as a squash and the hand of the king's daughter in marriage.

Of course, the four counselors were instructed to claim that all stories told were indeed true. No matter how preposterous the tale, the counselors always nodded their heads at its end and agreed, "Yes, yes, that could be true."

Now there was in this country a poor orphan boy who worked on a farm near the palace. Every day he saw men leaving the palace with dejected expressions. One day, the orphan boy asked a man "Oh, my Uncle, why do you look so very sad?" "This is because I have been tricked unfairly by the king and his counselors. I entered the king's lying contest. I told such a lie that no one could possibly believe it as truth. Yet when I had finished, the king's four counselors all swore that "Yes, this could be true. Had

I won, I would have received a reward of gold and the hand of the princess in marriage. This is so unfair."

The boy thought about this man's story for some time. He asked around and discovered that the king had cheated many storytellers in just this way. It was time to teach this king a lesson. When the orphan boy had finished his planting, he asked the old farmer for whom he worked if he would please present him at the palace. The old man found this an unusual request, but at last agreed to take the boy to the king.

As they entered the palace, they found the king surrounded by his courtiers. When the king heard that the boy wanted to enter the contest, he was delighted. "Excellent! It has been several days since I heard a good story. Begin at once." And the king and his court all settled back to listen to this new amusement.

The boy approached the front of the chamber and began his story. "Once upon a time, a long, long time ago ... I cannot tell you how long ago because I was not born yet, there lived a boy who earned his living working on a farm. This boy tended the water buffalo. He worked in the rice fields. The boy worked very hard. But one day, he heard that the king had opened a storytelling competition. A lying contest had been set with a great prize for the winner. The boy set out for the palace to enter that contest. But the way was so long that the boy became tired. He stopped in the shade of a large tree to rest.

"While the boy rested, he saw a herd of five elephants bathing in a nearby marsh. Suddenly, the boy had an idea. It would be much easier to travel by elephant than on foot! The way to the king's palace was very long. Why not ride an elephant there?

"The boy jumped to his feet and ran to catch one of the elephants. But the elephants saw him coming and fled in fear. The boy was not daunted. That boy followed them. He pursued them, running swiftly. The elephants saw the boy gaining on them, so they quickly climbed into the trees to escape. But that boy did not stop. That boy followed them. He climbed into the trees right after those elephants. The elephants were terrified. They looked down

9

from their treetop perches, and seeing the river flowing by below, the elephants jumped into its waters. That boy followed them.

"The boy jumped right into the water after them. The elephants were swept downstream. Struggling to stay afloat, they were carried right out into the wide ocean. That boy followed them. He swam determinedly after them.

"Suddenly, a sailing ship full of rough brigands appeared. The elephants were terrified. What if the sailors captured them and imprisoned them on board the ship? To escape such a cruel fate, the five elephants dived down beneath the ship, into the depths of the ocean. For three days and three nights they swam underwater. At last the ship had passed and it was safe to surface again. And that boy? That boy followed them! He dived right after them and did not let them out of his sight once for those three days and three nights.

"And so this chase continued. Sometimes on land, sometimes under the water, sometimes even in the air. Years passed. Decades passed. Still the elephants fled from the boy. And still that boy followed those elephants."

At this point, the orphan boy who was telling this preposterous tale stopped and looked around at his audience. The counselors, the courtiers, the king were all leaning forward expectantly. They were completely entranced by this boy's fabulous story. "Go on ... go on ... what happened then?" But the king shook his head, "Well if the elephants were fleeing all of the time, and the boy was pursuing, what were they eating during all of these years?"

The boy smiled. "Even I, the storyteller, cannot figure out how this story could be true. These elephants had been on the run since the boy was a child. Some say that during the chase that boy had grown into a young man, then into an old man. Now he could hardly walk. He had to crawl. And still he pursued those five elephants. He asked his children to carry him in the pursuit. Some say the elephants also had grown old. They were exhausted. They had left many baby elephants in the forest along the way. Still they fled and did not know how to stop.

"But maybe that part is not true, because in the end I know there were still just five elephants fleeing and one boy pursuing.

"One day, the five elephants were so tired that they could go no further. They took refuge in a small thatched hut, hiding from the boy. Still that boy followed. He caught them at last, right in that tiny hut. There was nothing the five elephants could do. Quickly, all five jumped into a teakettle to hide. But, alas, the boy had seen them. He jumped right in after them. Now there was only one means of escape ... through the spout! All five of those elephants tried to squeeze through that tiny spout at once. It was impossible! The boy seized all five by the tails. At last he had caught those elephants!

"So the triumphant boy rode his five elephants into this city. As he entered the city he met four counselors, the very four who sit in judgment on my story today. These counselors were so impressed with the elephants that each wanted to buy one for himself. The price of the elephants was high, 20 million *baht*! But the counselors readily agreed to pay it. So the boy sold an elephant to each of these counselors. The king himself bought the remaining elephant. All promised to pay the boy at a later date.

"Now many years have passed. That boy has returned to collect his payment. I am that boy. Today, I have come to collect the 20 million *baht* from each counselor and from the king. This is the payment I am owed for the sale of my five elephants. My story is at an end. Will the counselors and the king please give judgment on my story now? If it is true, please pay the money you owe to me. If it is false, bring out my reward and the princess!"

The Liars Contest of the King

Chapter 2

Nithan Talok: Humorous Tales

Drinking with Yommaban, the King of the Dead

Yommaban (Yomm-a-bän) is King of the Underworld. Written in his Book of Fate is the name and age of death of every person whose life he must reap. In Thai philosophy, there is no particular inconsistency in enjoying the Hindu pantheon of heavenly and otherworldly gods, such as Yommaban, even though the Thai are devout Buddhists.

There was a man who loved to drink whiskey. It was his habit to drink whiskey every day until he became drunk. When he was really drunk, he did not know what was going on around him. He wasn't even aware of the mosquitoes swarming around to bite him. And he wasn't aware that those poor mosquitoes became drunk themselves just from drinking his alcohol-laden blood!

This man had a wife and several children. There was only one thing that he really wanted in this life. He kept saying, "Before I die, I want to see my son ordained as a monk." Nothing else seemed to matter to this man, except for his whiskey. He even told his wife, "When I die, don't bother to do merit for me. I wouldn't even care. Just remember to put a bottle of whiskey in the coffin with me. *That* is important."

The time arrived when his son came of age. He could now become an ordained monk. The man was glad that this happy day was finally at hand. He told his wife to prepare for his son's ordination. But before the ceremony could occur, this drunken man died. His wife grieved, but as he had wished, she dutifully laid one bottle of whiskey in the coffin with his corpse.

As his spirit lifted from his body, the dead drunkard snatched the bottle of whiskey from the coffin and carried it with him on his way to hell.

Yommaban, the King of the Dead, greeted the new arrival. "During your life have you done many good deeds? Have you gained any merits?"

The man shook his head. "No, Sir. I never bothered myself with making merits. I just spent my time drinking whiskey." He opened the bottle and took a big drink, right in front of the King of the Dead.

The smell of that whiskey tickled the nose of the King of the Dead. He was curious. "What is it about this whiskey that makes you want to drink it all the time? Does it taste so good?"

The drunkard nodded. He poured some for Yommaban. "If you do not believe my words, sample some yourself. Whiskey is man's best friend. Whiskey is always faithful to man. The more you drink, the more drunk you become. The less you drink, the less drunk you are. If you do not drink, you do not have to urinate as often. If you drink a lot, be prepared to relieve yourself. Whiskey can be depended on."

The King of the Dead was curious. He wanted to see whether this man told the truth. Yommaban, King of the Dead, sat down and took a drink of the whiskey. It tasted bad, but still there was something about it. Yommaban drank some more. There they sat, the King of the Dead and this drunkard, talking and drinking until the bottle was empty.

Suddenly the man remembered his past and started to cry. Yommaban was confused. "Now, what? You just finished drinking your whiskey. Why do you cry ?"

"I am thinking of my son," said the man. "I will not be able to attend his ordination ceremony. I wanted to see my son enter the monkhood. Everything is already prepared. If only I could see my son become a monk, I would not feel sorry to die."

Yommaban was pleased to learn that the man told the truth and that he still believed in religion, even though he had not bothered to acquire merit in his life. Yommaban pulled out his record book and checked the drunkard's status. He found that this man was only 40 years old. Well, he could spare him a bit more time on earth. What would that hurt?

Yommaban spoke to his drinking partner. "I hate to see you cry like this. I feel sorry for you. Look, why don't I send you back to earth for one more year, so you can see your son ordained into the monkhood. I will send somebody to pick you up and bring you back down here afterward. You are 40 now. Here, I will just add a "1" to your score. What is one more year between friends, eh? By the way, you might bring along another bottle of whiskey when you come back down."

Yommaban drunkenly scratched a "1" in his record book and slammed it shut. Calling one of his assistants, he had the drunkard escorted back to earth.

The man recovered from his death. He told his wife all about his agreement with Yommaban. Then he prepared everything for his son's ordination. Once the son was ordained into the monkhood, the man relaxed. Now he had only to settle back with his whiskey bottle and wait for Yommaban to send for him again. As the year drew to an end, the man began to drink more whiskey than ever. But the anniversary of his death passed and Yommaban did not send for him. A second year passed. Still, the man lived on. Ten, 20, 30, 40 years passed. The man was becoming very old. He felt miserable all of the time. He didn't even feel like drinking any more. "Why doesn't Yommaban come for me?" he wondered. "Am I to go on existing in this state of miserable old age forever?"

Meanwhile, Yommaban, himself, was puzzled. It seemed much longer than a year since that drunkard with the whiskey bottle had visited. Why hadn't he returned? Yommaban pulled out his record book and turned to the man's name. "Well now I understand about this drinking business," he said. "No wonder whiskey is said to be bad for you. It must really fog your mind. I,

Yommaban, who have never made a mistake before, actually *made a mistake!*" There in the record book was the man's original death age, clearly written "40." And beside it was scrawled a "1", the "1" that a drunken Yommaban had added. The man's age of death now read "401."

Sri Thanonchai and the King

The stories of Sri Thanonchai (See Ta-non-chai), the clever trickster, are told throughout Thailand. In some areas, he is known as Siengmieng (Siangmiang), and in this tale Sri Thanonchai is addressed by the honorable term "Phra Sri" (Pra Se), as his status as a high ranking government official requires. But, whatever his name, his antics are the same.

One day, the king was strolling in the royal gardens with his courtesans and courtiers. As they reached a garden pond, the king, thinking to challenge Sri Thanonchai's wit, taunted him. "You are brainy, Sri Thanonchai. Can you think of a way to make your king go into this pond?"

Phra Sri answered, "Your Majesty, I could not persuade you to get into this water. That I could not do. But I could certainly make you come *out* of the water. I guarantee that with my life, sir."

"Let us see." And the king quickly took off his clothes and lowered himself into the pond. Floating in the water, he asked. "Now, Phra Sri. Start talking. How will you make me come out of this water?"

Phra Sri laughed. Bowing politely to the king, he said. "Dear Majesty, I was not attempting to make you come out of the pond. I was attempting to make you go *into* the pond. And as you can see, I have succeeded!"

"Sri Thanonchai, you are too clever!" exclaimed the king. He came out of the water graciously, pleased with the wit of Sri Thanonchai.

Sri Thanonchai and the Two Moons

Once Phra Sri borrowed money from an old woman named Sa (Sä). "I cannot believe that a wealthy man like you lacks money," said the old woman jokingly.

"Even a millionnaire can lack a match some times," smiled Phra Sri.

"How long will it be before you return this money?" asked the old woman.

"When two full moons have come," said Phra Sri.

Two months passed, twice the full moon came and went. And Phra Sri did not return the borrowed money.

The old woman came to his house and said: "Two months have already passed, Phra Sri. Two full moons have come and gone. I would like to have my money returned."

"Not yet, two moons have not come yet," argued Phra Sri. The old woman thought she might be wrong. She went home and waited. Many more months passed. Still Phra Sri did not return the money. The old woman came again to the house and said: "It must be more than two full moons now. I would like to have my money back."

"No, it is not two moons yet," argued Phra Sri.

This went on for a year. Finally, the old lady told Phra Sri, "I will have to take you to court, Phra Sri. You have borrowed my money and will not return it."

"As you like, old woman," said Phra Sri without worrying. "Even if you take me to court, you will lose, because it is not two full moons yet."

"Why do you keep saying that? It is a new year already," said the old woman.

"But it is true," explained Phra Sri. "There is only one moon in the sky. Even though time has passed, I still see only one moon when I look up. I told you I would return the money when there were two moons, did I not?"

The old lady was stunned and weary. She cried out loud: "You are not fair. You tricked me. I will not give this up." She left the house, crying all the way home. She intended to take the matter to court.

Then, along the way, she met a Buddhist novice. The novice asked her, "Old woman, why are you crying? Are you in trouble? Are you lost?" When the old woman had told him the story, the novice said, "Do not trouble yourself about this. I will represent you in court. We can easily win this case."

When the day of the trial came, the novice appeared before the judge and asked that the trial be postponed until evening when the full moon would be visible. That night, after it was dark, the novice led the judge, the old woman, and Sri Thanonchai to a small pond behind the court. The novice pointed upward to the sky. "See, there is the full moon. One moon." Then he pointed downward to the moon's reflection in the pond. "See, there is another moon. Two moons. The time has arrived for Sri Thanonchai to pay his debt."

Sri Thanonchai could not believe his eyes. Here were the two moons. He did not know how to respond. This is one time when the clever trickster was tricked.

Sri Thanonchai's Special Dishes

Khun Muang (Khoon Mooung) was a minister in the king's cabinet. This was an important position, and he carried it well. But he was constantly being embarrassed by his wife. This woman had a very foul mouth. She would open it and let out the most horrendous stream of curses. She was constantly finding something to whine or complain about. So it took very little provocation for her to break into a string of curses that would embarrass everyone within earshot.

One day, Khun Muang spoke to Sri Thanonchai in private. "I have a problem I have been unable to solve, Sri Thanonchai."

"What is it, sir?"

"It's my wife. She speaks so rudely. Her tirades are very unpleasant to the ears. I have to close my ears to keep out her raucous complaining," explained Khun Muang.

"If you close your ears to keep her voice out, where does it go?" quipped Sri Thanonchai.

"Oh it worms its way in all right," said Khun Muang. "But nobody likes to hear such rude words and whines. Some days she keeps up all day long with her cursing and complaining. Her mouth opens, shuts, opens, shuts, like a flashing furnace. It is painful to be around her."

"Why do you tell me this, sir?" asked Sri Thanonchai.

"Isn't there some way you could make my wife change her behavior? I would like for her to become more polite in her speech, to speak only sweet words, and to utter sounds that are pleasant to the ears. Is this possible?"

"This is very simple, sir," answered Sri Thanonchai. "Let me work in your home as a servant for a while. I will soon find a way to give your wife a lesson in manners."

So Sri Thanonchai was brought to Khun Muang's house as a servant. Sensing his tricky nature, Khun Muang's wife took an instant dislike to him. To make matters worse, he was obviously one of Khun Muang's favorites.

One evening when Khun Muang's wife had finished cooking dinner, Khun Muang did not arrive to eat it. The cabinet meeting had continued longer than usual. They were still debating some difficult matter. Lady Khun Muang was enraged that her husband would keep her waiting. She sent Sri Thanonchai to go fetch Khun Muang. "Tell him to come at once, before his food is spoiled!" she shouted.

Sri Thanonchai decided to pass the message on just as it was given. He ran straight to the royal court, stood outside the door, and shouted at the top of his lungs: "Khun Muang! Khun Muang! Your wife wants you to come home right now and eat your dinner, sir."

Sri Thanonchai kept hollering like this until a very embarrassed Khun Muang excused himself and hurried out. The cabinet members laughed and called a halt to their meeting. "Better run along now Khun Muang. Your *wife* is waiting." "We'd better stop our meeting *right now*. Khun Muang's *wife* doesn't approve."

As Khun Muang's house was near the cabinet hall, his wife could hear Sri Thanonchai's shouting. She felt embarrassed. "Why did you shout so?" she reprimanded Sri Thanonchai when he returned.

"I had to shout, my lady. I had to stop that cabinet meeting right away so Khun Muang would come."

"But it is embarrassing. The others were laughing at me."

"My lady, you should not feel embarrassed. Now people know that Khun Muang's wife cares about him. She is concerned that he might not eat on time. Anyway, the other cabinet members were hungry too and were glad that the meeting stopped."

This answer pleased Lady Khun Muang.

That night Sri Thanonchai came in secret to meet with Khun Muang. "You know, sir, your wife has good manners. She really knows what is suitable and what is not. When I shouted today, she realized that it was not polite. I think she is well-mannered under it all." Lady Khun Muang was hiding behind the door listening. She heard this compliment and was pleased. She did not know that Sri Thanonchai had planned for her to overhear him.

"I am still not pleased," complained Khun Muang. "She is a good wife and a good cook. In fact, her only bad quality is her foul mouth."

"This is not so bad, sir," said Sri Thanonchai. "And she may learn to improve her foul-mouthed nature."

Lady Khun Muang heard all this. She decided to improve. She wanted her husband to be proud of her. The next evening she asked Sri Thanonchai, "You seem to be capable at everything you do. Do you cook as well?"

"Sri Thanonchai is an excellent cook," interjected Khun Muang.

"In that case, perhaps I could learn from you," said Lady Khun Muang. "Would you prepare a dish for us?"

"I would be glad to prepare my special recipe for you. But I must go to the market for the ingredients," said Sri Thanonchai.

The next morning at breakfast, everybody was eagerly waiting at the table to see what Sri Thanonchai's special dish would be. Every dish on the table was covered. Lady Khun Muang uncovered the first dish expectantly. Her eyes bulged out at what she saw. She uncovered the second dish. Her nose wrinkled. When she uncovered the third dish, her mouth dropped open in surprise. And when she uncovered the fourth dish, she could not contain herself. "What on earth did you cook, Sri Thanonchai?"

"These are my special dishes. The most delicious dishes in the world, my lady."

But there is nothing here but *tongue*! Cow tongue. Buffalo tongue. Pig tongue. Duck tongue. Chicken tongue. Fish tongue. They are not even seasoned. Just plain, boiled tongue!"

"But tongue is the most important organ, my lady. Remember the old saying. 'The human tongue is the most important organ. You will know if a thing is tasty or not by your tongue. If your tongue speaks pleasant words, the listeners will savour that taste until the day they die.' That is why the tongue is the most delicious dish.

Sugar cane or sugar palm may be sweet when you eat it, but once you swallow, the sweetness is gone. But the sweetness of a pleasantly speaking tongue is a remembered sweetness that lasts forever. Is this not true, Khun Muang?" asked Sri Thanonchai.

"Yes, that is true."

Lady Khun Muang knew right away that she was being given a lesson. She was annoyed, but could not find any words to answer in this circumstance.

Khun Muang told Sri Thanonchai, "Well, today you cooked your most tasty dishes. Why don't you show us your most untasty dishes for tomorrow. If *these* are tasty, I am curious to see what your *unsavory* dishes would be."

The next day, the food on the table was covered again. When the dishes were uncovered, what did they see? Tongue, tongue, and tongue again! Boiled without spices. "Sri Thanonchai, what is the meaning of this? Boiled tongue *again*?" Lady Khun Muang was furious.

"Madame, it is the human tongue which is most sweet. But it is also the human tongue which can taste most foul. The tongue which gives forth bad language, bad breath, and rude and insulting words. The tongue which lets slip gossip, whines, and complaints. When we hear curses and foul language, all who hear become sad, angry, or hurt by that human tongue. Tongue is certainly the most foul dish I could prepare."

Lady Khun Muang understood. She decided this might be the time to change her ways. Because she was the lady of the house, no one had been able to correct her ways, and her mouth had become fouler and fouler. Now Sri Thanonchai had shown her indirectly just what the results of her speech might be. She realized that her ugly speaking habits were affecting others. From that day, Lady Khun Muang thought before she spoke. She tried to use pleasant words and kind phrases. She became a model of gentleness and civility.

Chapter 3

Nithan Ruang Sat: Animal Tales

Why the Bear Has a Short Tail

This Thai story explains why bears have short tails, and also includes an ending explaining the building of the kok bird's nest. This bird is allowed to bring soil from three cities together to build its nest. This reflects the honor accorded the King of Thailand, who mixes the waters of three rivers for ceremonial purposes. Kok birds are especially intriguing to the Thai because their couples bond for life. It is believed that if either is killed, the mate will fly high into the sky and then plummet to the earth, committing suicide to join its mate in death.

Once upon a time, in a wide forest, many animals lived together. Among the four-footed animals, Bear prided himself as the most powerful one. Among the families of birds, Kok Bird was considered the most powerful. Kok Bird had a bigger body and a bigger beak than any other bird. Kok Bird had strong, wide wings that enabled him to fly long distances without tiring.

Though Kok Bird was clearly strongest of the birds, and Bear was clearly strongest of the animals, these two were constantly in conflict. They could not establish which of them was most powerful. At last, they challenged each other to a competition. All the animals were called together to witness the outcome. On the day of the contest, the animals arrived excitedly. Some perched in the tops of the trees, others stayed on the lower branches, some crowded themselves on the ground. All cheered loudly as Bear and Kok Bird appeared.

Bear climbed to the top of the tallest tree and waited for the signal to begin. Kok Bird flew to the uppermost branch and perched there gracefully.

When the appointed time arrived, Bear stood up and announced loudly. "Now begins the contest between Kok Bird and myself, Bear. You can all witness for yourselves who is the most powerful animal in this forest. We will compete by shouting as loud as we can. Whoever has the loudest voice will win."

Bear and Kok Bird chose lots and it was decided that Bear should try first. Now, at that time Bear had a long, bushy tail. He stood up slowly, and proudly let his lovely long tail trail down over the branch. When the wind blew, Bear's tail moved gracefully against the wind. It was a beautiful sight.

Bear announced, "Dear Fellow Animals, now I am going to shout. I suggest that those of you who are easily frightened hold on to branches or rocks tightly. Those birds who are perched on the tallest branches, be especially careful of falling. I further suggest that Kok Bird hold onto the branch of this tree with his beak. Because you are so close to me, Kok Bird, you will be affected the most."

The animals, hearing Bear's boastful claim and observing his scare tactics, were not pleased. They felt sliced by Bear's threat. As for Kok Bird, he smiled good-naturedly and stood still. When everything and everyone was ready, Bear shouted as loud as he could. His roar was so loud that it spread through the forest. All of the animals were impressed by Bear's loud voice.

When Bear had finished shouting three times as agreed, he came back to his place on top of the tallest tree. He felt sure that he would win. He would be King of the Forest. The other animals gossiped among themselves. "Bear may win. His noise was so loud that it almost deafened my ears!"

When his turn came, Kok Bird walked to the end of the branch where he perched. He, too, announced clearly to the other animals, "Dear Fellow Animals, now it is my turn to shout. Please remain comfortably wherever you are. There is nothing to fear. However, I do suggest that the great, brave Bear use his beautiful, bushy, long tail to tie himself to the branch. Otherwise, Bear, you might get hurt falling."

Bear disregarded Kok Bird's warning. He thought to himself, "I will not do as Kok Bird tells me." Kok Bird stretched his neck and spread his broad wings. Those wings stirred violently, making the air roar. Branches of the trees moved back and forth wildly. Bear was not prepared. He almost fell. Quickly, Bear grasped tightly onto one of the waving branches. Kok Bird laughed and said, "You see! If I shout and you do not use your tail to tie yourself to the tree, your life may be in danger. And do not blame me that I did not tell you so! I will not guarantee your safety."

Bear began to realize that Kok Bird spoke the truth. He was sitting on top of the tallest tree in the forest. If he fell ... hurriedly, Bear used his beautiful, bushy tail to tie himself to a branch. When Bear was ready, Kok Bird shouted again, loudly. The voice of Kok Bird echoed throughout that forest, then on to the next valley, and the next, and the next.

All the animals who had gathered were excited. They proclaimed noisily that they had never heard such a voice before. They had not imagined that Kok Bird could shout so loudly.

Kok Bird smiled contentedly, saying, "I will shout again for you, Dear Fellow Animals, and for the Great Bear, so that he can be sure of my voice." Then Kok Bird shouted again. The voice echoed again everywhere throughout the valleys. After a long time, the voice could still be heard echoing on throughout the distant forest. Bear, hearing such a powerful, loud voice, was so scared that he fainted and fell down from the tallest tree. Because of his weight and the height of the tree, his beautiful, bushy tail, still tied to the branch, was torn.

It was agreed that the Kok Bird was King of the Forest. "In honor of this occasion," said the animals, "your family may choose for their nests the soil of three different cities." As for Bear, he was beaten. His beautiful, bushy tail was torn so short and scraggly that it gradually disappeared altogether and today he has only a very small bit of a tail.

Why the Bear Has a Short Tail

That evening, after all of the other animals had left, Kok Bird's relatives gathered together. His father, mother, brothers and sisters, and all of his cousins came. Kok Bird said to them, "Dear Father, Mother, and every one of you, I personally thank you for your help in echoing my voice throughout the valleys and the forests today. It is you who have helped me win the contest. To commemorate our victory, from now on let us build our nest by using soil from three different cities."

Since that day Kok Bird has been known as the King of the Forest. And since then, all kok birds are entitled to bring soil from three different cities to build their nest. This was possible because the kok birds were united, ready to help each other.

Tiger Seeks Wisdom

Though the farmer's wisdom in this tale consists mostly of his cleverness, the Thai term *panya* (pän-yä) implies a deep, insightful knowledge as well. *Panya* is a highly desirable quality.

At the edge of the forest, near a mountain, lived a farmer. Every day he worked hard plowing his field. One day, after he had worked hard all morning, the farmer stopped to go home for his lunch.

On the mountain, a tiger had been watching this farmer. The farmer's plow was pulled by a strong buffalo. That buffalo obeyed the farmer's every whim, yet the buffalo seemed strong, with long, sharp horns. Why did this huge animal let the puny farmer put a rope around its nose? The tiger decided to investigate.

The tiger came down from its mountain and made straight for the buffalo. The poor buffalo thought the tiger meant to attack, and prepared to defend itself, but the tiger greeted the buffalo amicably. "Friend, I come in peace. Do not panic. I am your friend, not your enemy."

The buffalo spoke guardedly, "What is your business with me?"

The tiger asked, "I am curious. Why do you work for this man? He is much smaller and weaker than you. Working in the field like this is hard work. Why do it? You are bigger and stronger than man. Surely you must be able to overpower him?"

The buffalo shook his head. "My friend, how can I harm man? Even though he is smaller and weaker, man has something which I lack. Man has *panya*. I must be his servant. He is more clever than I."

The tiger, hearing that, wondered what this *panya* could be. "What is this *panya*? I have never seen it. What does it look like?"

The buffalo laughed. "If you want to know what *panya* is, you should ask man himself. He will be back soon."

So the tiger walked over to the forest edge and waited for man to return.

The farmer had finished his lunch. He put his knife at his waist. He smoked his cigar. He chewed his tobacco leaves. Then he hurried back to the field. He wanted to finish his work before the plowing season was over.

When the farmer saw the tiger blocking his way, he was terrified. He pulled the knife from his waist and prepared to defend himself. But the tiger spoke, "Sir, do not be afraid. Please put your knife down. I will not harm you. I was waiting to ask you a question. I have been told that you have a special thing called *panya*. I would like to see what this *panya* looks like."

Hearing this, the farmer knew right away what to do. He said, "Dear Tiger! I forgot to bring *panya* with me. I left it back at my home."

The tiger really wanted to see this *panya*, so he begged the farmer, "Would you mind going home to get it? Just bring your *panya* back and let me see what it looks like."

"I do not dare go home, " said the farmer, "and leave you here with my buffalo. You, a tiger, might kill my buffalo before I return."

The tiger pleaded once more. "Dear Farmer, I promise I will not kill your buffalo. If you do not trust me, you can tie me to this tree. Then you will know that I cannot harm your buffalo. Please go home and bring back your *panya*."

The farmer, with seeming reluctance, agreed to this plan. With a stout rope he tied the tiger tightly to a large tree. Then the farmer used his knife to cut two big sticks. With these sticks he beat the poor tiger mercilessly, saying "Foolish Tiger. Pray for your life now. This is what you wanted to see. This is *panya*. Now you know what wisdom is."

The Elephants and the Bees

Working elephants are a common sight in Northern Thailand. For another story about elephants, see "The Good Boy" in this collection. This story tells of an earlier time, when elephants roamed free.

There was a time when elephants did not have long noses as they do now. In those days, elephants had to travel far to find their food. They never stayed at one place for long.

At this same time, there lived a swarm of bees that had built its hive on a low branch of a tree near the forest. Every day, those bees went out to collect honey from the flowers in the area.

One year, the weather became so dry that all the leaves dried up and fell from the trees. The poor elephants could not find anything to eat. Food was scarce. Vegetables and leaves could not grow because of the lack of water. Even the bees were starving.

Then one day, a forest fire started and spread rapidly through the dry forest. The elephants ran away as fast as they could. But they could find no safe shelter. Closer and closer came the fire. Then the elephants saw the bees buzzing ahead of them. Perhaps these flying insects could help them. When the bees realized that the huge elephants were asking *them* for aid they laughed. Then they said, "Yes, we can tell you about a safe shelter from the fire. But you must help us in return."

The elephants agreed. To their surprise, the bees asked the elephants to open their huge mouths. Then the bees flew right inside the elephant's noses. They *stayed* there. From this safe hiding place, the bees directed the elephants. They guided them to a large pond. "Go right into the middle of the pond. Do not move until the fire has passed on."

The elephants did just as the bees suggested. Standing in the pond for several days, they waited until the fire had burned itself out. All the trees of the forest were burnt away. But the elephants and the bees had survived.

Now the elephants emerged from the pond and called to the bees to come on out of their noses and mouths.

But the bees liked living in that spot. They refused to come out! Those elephants were so angry. *"Prae Praen! Prae Praen!"* they trumpeted. They shook their heavy heads from side to side. They blew hard on their noses. Harder and harder they blew, trying to blow those bees out. And the harder they blew, the longer their noses became! But the bees would not come out. And all of their blowing and trumpeting served only to make their poor noses very, very long.

Now the elephants decided they could rid themselves of those pesky bees with fire. After all, the bees had flown into the elephant's noses and mouths in the first place in order to escape fire. So lighting a fire, the elephants began to inhale the smoke. Opening their mouths they breathed deeply, then shut their mouths tightly and held that smoke inside. It worked. The bees could not stand that smoke. They flew hurriedly from the noses of those elephants.

But now that the bees had become accustomed to living in such a warm dark hole, they looked for a similar place to live. Since then these bees build their homes only in hollow trees. They are called *Phung Phrong* bees, which means "the hole like an elephant's mouth." But to get their honeycombs is easy, you simply smoke them out. They are still afraid of fire!

As for the elephants, they were glad to be rid of those bees. But they feared another infestation, so to make sure their noses and mouths were kept free of bees, they began to swallow water and blow it out through their noses. To this day they keep that habit. And it is a very good technique, too, for making sure your nose is free of bees!

Power and Wisdom

This Thai tale is a direct transplant from India. It is found in the ancient collection of Indian legendry, *The Panchatantra*.

A long long time ago, in a deep forest, there lived a lion who claimed to be King of the Animals. He ruled over all the other animals. One day, wanting to show off his power, he demanded that all the animals gather for a meeting.

When the animals had arrived, Lion announced, "Dear Animals, as you know, I am the Greatest Animal, the Most Powerful One. If you did not have me to rule over you, you and your offspring might be bothered by other, foreign animals. You might not be able to live as peacefully as you do today." Lion stopped speaking to let his words sink in, then he went on, "All day long, I have to stay in this cave. I must act as judge for you when you quarrel. I do not have time to go out into the forest and look for food. Therefore, from now on, I want you to take turns bringing me my food. Every one of you must share this responsibility. If any of you do not do as I ask, I will have to deal with you personally."

The animals, on hearing Lion's command, did not know what to do. If they refused, they would surely be killed by Lion. Reluctantly, they agreed to his decree. Each animal would take a turn bringing food to Lion.

When Rabbit's turn came, he was not happy. Rabbit hated to be forced into serving the king. Still, he could not think of a safe way to get out of this duty. Then, while resting in a large cave, Rabbit noticed something. A pond lay at the back of the cave. Peering over the rocky cliff edge into the pond, Rabbit saw another timid rabbit peering back. It was Rabbit's own reflection. Suddenly Rabbit had a plan.

It was late by the time Rabbit approached Lion's cave, and Lion roared hungrily when he saw the tiny Rabbit coming. "Why are you so late? And where is my food?"

Rabbit bowed respectfully to Lion. "Oh Dear Sir Lion, Oh Great and Powerful One! I was late because as I walked hurriedly this way, I was stopped by another lion. This lion told me that *he* is the greatest, most powerful animal in the forest. He told me I must bring food to *him*, not to you. He challenges you to a fight at once to determine who is the stronger. He is waiting for you now, in a big cave."

Lion was furious at such a challenge. He roared so loudly that the forest shook and all the animals trembled. "Take me to that lion right away. I will prove to all animals that I, myself, am the Most Powerful One!"

Rabbit did not hesitate. He hurriedly led Lion to the big cave. At the front of the cave Rabbit stopped. In seeming trepidation, he begged, "Please Sir Lion, Oh Powerful One, I am so afraid of that other lion. Do not make me face him again. Go in by yourself. The other lion is at the end of the cave."

Then Rabbit ran quickly away, leaving Lion by himself at the cave entrance. Lion did not hesitate. He ran straight into the cave. Reaching the end of the cave, he looked down and saw another lion standing just as tall and proud as he!

Lion roared furiously and bared his teeth. The other lion did exactly the same! This lion *mocked* him! His roar echoed loudly in the cave. Lion was infuriated. He pounced onto that roaring lion below, intending to rip him to shreds. Instead, he found himself sinking into a deep pool of water. That was the end of the regal lion. Never again did the animals have to sacrifice their food to the whims of a "king."

Chapter 4

Nithan Chadok: Jataka Tales

The Deer Buddha

    The *Jataka* tales, *Chadok* (shä-dok) in Thai, are stories telling of the actions of Buddha in previous lives. Each of these tales shows his qualities of mercy, self-sacrifice, and wisdom. The *Jataka* are used as teaching tales by the Buddhist monks. Other stories exemplifying these same qualities have also been told by the monks over the centuries. These too may be known as *Chadok*.

    In a previous life of Our Lord Buddha, the Buddha, in his deer form, was the leader of a herd of deer. The leader of another herd of deer in the same forest was Thewathat (Taw-a-tut). Each herd contained 500 deer. Both herds roamed in the forest of *Isi-patanamarukhathaiyawan* (I-si-p-a-t-a-n-a-m-a-r-u-k-a-ti-ya-wan), the Deer Forest.

    In those days, the King of *Parannasi* (Pä-rä-nna-se), who lived nearby, loved to hunt. He always hunted in that Deer Forest. On each hunt, he and his soldiers would kill many deer.

    One day, the King of Parannasi met the Deer Buddha as he was hunting in the forest. The Deer Buddha approached the king and spoke: "Your majesty, every day you and your soldiers come to this forest to hunt. You have killed hundreds of deer with your arrows. If this continues, my friends will all be destroyed and there will be no more deer in this forest. There will be no more prey for you to hunt in the future. Notice also that the deer you do shoot with your arrows are all hungry, thin, and frightened. They have been hiding from you in the forest and could not come to look for food. They have not dared come out into the open for fear that you might shoot them with your arrows. Even though you kill many deer, their meat is thin and tough.

"I have a proposal for your majesty. Let us live longer and live in peace. Do not slaughter many of us each day. If you need meat, kill only one deer. Let the others browse for their food without being frightened. If you allow our deer to eat in peace, they will not be so thin and hungry. I promise to send you one deer each day. You will receive a deer who is fat and tender for your food. And you will be known as the king who is kind, the king who has saved the deer from extinction in this forest."

The King of Parannasi agreed with the wisdom of the Deer Buddha. He ordered his soldiers back to town. From then on, he hunted every day, but he needed only one arrow to kill his one deer. Everything was as the Deer Buddha had promised. The Deer Buddha and Thewathat took turns selecting the daily deer from their herds. If the king did not come hunting in the forest on that day, the deer was instructed to go to the town gate and wait for the soldiers who would come out and slaughter it. Though it was hard to die, that chosen deer felt good, knowing that its sacrifice enabled its people to live in peace.

All went as planned until one day it became the time of a young doe to be killed. She was nearing the time to bear a child and was so sad that her baby would die when she herself was killed.

The doe went to Thewathat, the herd's leader and pleaded. "Dear Thewathat, my leader, I know that it is my turn to be killed by the king. I am willing to be killed, but I am soon to have a baby. I beg you to let me have my baby first. Then I will gladly go to be killed."

Thewathat would not oblige her. The doe tried again and again to change his mind, asking for mercy for the sake of the unborn deer. But he would not agree. He told her: "I cannot let you escape your duty. It is your turn to become prey for the King of Parannasi. You must go. Tomorrow, you are to place yourself where the king comes to hunt."

The poor doe asked other deer from the herd to take her place, but no other deer would volunteer to die for her.

At last, desperation drove her to the Deer Buddha, leader of the other herd. She begged the Deer Buddha to help her postpone her death until the baby could be born.

Lord Buddha the Deer pitied her. He felt touched by the love this mother deer held for her unborn child. He said: "I understand your love for your baby. A mother's love is so great that she will do anything for her child. Nothing can compare to the love of a mother for her children. I will help you with all my power. Go back to your home and be content. Take care of yourself and your unborn child. I will take care of everything else. Do not worry."

The next day, it was the Deer Buddha himself who appeared at the city's gate. When the citizens of Parannasi heard that the leader of the deer herd had come to be killed in the doe's place, they gathered to look at the deer king. They whispered among themselves. "It is not fair for this deer king to be killed. He is such a kind and graceful animal." Some said, "This beautiful deer should not be wasted. He should be fed and cared for as the pride of the land. He is such a graceful and lovely animal."

Others said: "This deer is kind and just. He is the one who asked the king not to slaughter the deer en masse. Why is he being killed? He does not deserve to be killed." Nobody wanted the Deer Buddha to be killed.

When the king heard this talk among the people, he went to the city's gate to see for himself. He was amazed to see that it really was the Deer Buddha. This handsome animal king was lying on the ground with his neck outstretched on the cutting block, waiting to be killed. The King of Parannasi approached the Deer Buddha and asked. "You are the leader of the herd, why do you have to come to be killed? If you die, who will lead your herd? You do not have to take a turn in this killing."

The Deer Buddha told the king about the young doe with her unborn baby. He explained his pity for her and her unborn child. He explained that she should have the chance to bear her baby and care for it before being killed.

The king began to realize the impact of his actions on the deer. He thought about this mother's love for her child. It was the same as a human's love. He had killed so many such mothers, so many young deer. He had separated so many families. He had caused so much grief. Now the king felt sorrow. He said, "Oh, Deer Buddha, King of all the Deer, I have a human body, but my mind is still animal, while you have an animal body, yet your heart is kind and thoughtful. It is you who are better than human beings such as I. I am ashamed. I am sorry. From now on, I will not kill deer. I give my word, there will be no more hunting. Your deer may roam the forest freely. You may eat in peace in my forest, for I will not let anyone destroy your people anymore. Please forgive me and be happy, for I will not hunt again."

Seven Stars

In this tale, a hen and her chicks pay the ultimate sacrifice and are rewarded by becoming a constellation, The Pleiades. Such tales stressing religious upbringing and self-sacrifice are classed as *Chadok* (shä-dok) in Thai folklore.

It is usual for monks to make their rounds of the neighborhood near their temple each morning with their begging bowls. Into these bowls the villagers place some rice and food for the monks' daily meal. The monks do not take food after noon each day, and they depend on the villagers for their food. By offering support to the monks, who look after the religious life of the community, the villagers acquire *merit* which will benefit them in future lives. Each person may acquire *merit* in this life by good deeds. The good things which occur to you in this life are the result of good deeds performed in past lives. Your misfortunes are the result of bad deeds. It is said "What belongs to you, will come to you." Looking to the future, devout Thai try to accumulate as much merit as possible.

There once was an old couple who lived in a small hut set in a grove of fruit trees. They tended their fruit trees, raised a few chickens, and survived. Both husband and wife were devout. They meditated often and each morning, when they arose, they would prepare some food to offer the monks.

But one evening the old woman seemed worried. "Dear Husband, what are we going to offer the monks tomorrow?"

Her husband was unconcerned, "Why do you worry over such a small matter. We have plenty of fruit on our trees, there are plenty of fish in the river, there is plenty of rice in the fields. Why worry?"

"Oh, my Dear Husband!" cried the old woman, "Didn't you notice? We have eaten all of the ripe fruit in our garden. Those fruits which are left are too small to eat. The bananas are just starting to grow. Some of the trees are only blooming. There is no fruit at all ripe enough to eat. Tomorrow, when the monk stops in front of our house, we will not have anything to offer him. There are not many people on our street who offer food for the monks."

"I see. You are worried that the monk may go hungry tomorrow."

"Yes, that is it. I am worried that tomorrow the monk may have no food to eat. He may have only water for his hunger. I do not want him to starve."

The old man was quiet for a while, then he slapped his leg and exclaimed. "I know what we can do. My Dear Wife, tomorrow we can kill our hen and use its meat to prepare food for the monk."

The old woman was shocked and reluctant. This hen was her pet. She did not want to kill it. Still, she did not want the monk to go hungry. The old man consoled her.

"Don't hesitate, my Dear Wife. We have good intentions in this. We have a good reason for killing our pet. We are making merit by offering food to the monk. It is a proper thing to do. We ourselves will not eat the chicken's meat at all."

Now the mother hen, who lived under the hut, heard all that was said between the old couple. She knew with certainty that she would be killed in the morning. She knew she must provide the food for the monk. This she could bear. But she cried for her six children.

"Kook! Kook! My children! Darlings. Listen to me carefully. I must teach you for the last time. Tomorrow, I am to be killed. This is necessary, in order that the old couple can provide food for the monk. Now listen and remember. Please love each other. Do not quarrel. Do not separate. Unite, all of you."

She was so distressed that she could not say anything else. The six children ran under the hen's wings and cried. "Oh, Mother, Dear Mother, how can we live without you?"

The hen embraced all six of her children. She told them lovingly, "Dears, tomorrow when they come to take me away, do not worry. Do not be sad. I will die for a good cause. You are still too small to go out alone into this world. Remember, do not wander too far from home. Beware of the eagle. Be careful, and do not play in the old couple's vegetable garden. Do not go into their hut or they will strike you. Be good children and look for your food under the hut and around the hut. Make yourselves loveable so that the old couple will want to keep you as their pets."

The mother hen taught her children until late that night. All the things that young chickens must know, she taught them. Then, as the sun rose, the mother hen embraced her six chicks and said, "Dears, please be good. I must go now to be killed so that the old couple can prepare my meat for the monk. Pray for me and pray that we will meet again as mother and daughters in our next lives. Pray that we will be born and live very long lives later. Because I am so willing to die for the monk and for our owners, I believe we will be granted our wish."

The mother hen began to walk away from them, but she ran back one more time to embrace each of her daughters. The six chicks sobbed quietly. They said, "Once our mother is dead, who is going to look after us? Who is going to teach us what to do and what not to do? Who is going to dry our tears?"

Upstairs, the old man and the old woman had risen early to prepare the fire and boil the water so they could cook the hen. As soon as the water was boiling, the old man came down to catch the hen. When the six chicks saw their mother plunged to her death in the boiling water, they could not contain themselves. They ran to the pot and jumping in after their mother, all six chicks died with her.

Because of their love for each other, because of their courageous act, because of their willingness to die so that their bodies could provide meat for the ordained monk, and because of their fervent wish to be born again as a family, these chicks and their mother were born again as stars. They became a constellation of seven stars and were placed together into the sky. At night you can see them high in the Thai sky. "*Dao Luk Kai,*" the "Seven Chicks" they are called. Look for them if ever you visit Thailand.

The Honest Woodcutter

This folktale, told throughout Asia, stresses the importance of honesty in one's dealings. *Rukkha* (Rook-kha) is the
Thai word for "tree." *Thewada* (Tay-wa-dä) means "god." Old
and venerable trees in Thailand are believed to serve as homes
for special tree spirits. Even young trees and plants *may* house
spirits, but old trees are almost certain to do so.

Once upon a time, there was a poor woodcutter who lived
near the edge of the forest. This woodcutter earned his living by
cutting firewood from the forest and selling it in the town. Every
day, he went into the forest to cut wood, everyday he carried his
cut firewood to the market to sell.

One day, the woodcutter was felling trees near a river. Somehow his axe slipped from his hand and flew right into the water.
The woodcutter did not know how to swim, and the river was
very deep at this point. He poked in the river with a long pole,
hoping to pull the lost axe out, but it was no use. The poor
woodcutter was desperate. "What should I do," he thought to
himself. "I cannot go back home empty-handed. Without my axe
I cannot cut any more firewood. Without firewood to sell, I will
have no money to buy food. I have no money to buy a new axe. I
must retrieve my axe, somehow. The woodcutter tried again to
dredge the axe from the river with a long pole. It was useless.
Becoming more and more desperate, the poor man sat down and
began to pray to the *Rukkha-thewada*, the tree spirit, for help.

Suddenly, a bright light issued from the huge tree. The *Rukkha-
thewada*, himself, was emerging from the tree. In the hand of the
Rukkha-thewada was a golden axe.

"Is this your axe, woodsman?"

The poor woodcutter looked at the axe. It was made of pure
gold! What a treasure. How wonderful it would be to own such a
lovely and valuable axe. Still, the woodcutter politely told the

Rukkha-thewada, "No, sir. That is not my lost axe. Mine is an ordinary axe."

The *Rukkha-thewada* waved his hand once. The golden axe disappeared and in its place a silver axe glistened. "Perhaps *this* is your lost axe?"

The poor woodcutter was tempted. The silver axe glistened in the sun. How wonderful it would be to own such a lovely and valuable axe. Still, the woodcutter politely told the *Rukkha-thewada*, "No, sir, that is not my lost axe."

The *Rukkha-thewada* waved his hand once more. The silver axe disappeared and in its place was an old, worn metal axe. "Is this your axe?"

The woodcutter was so pleased to see his old axe returned. "Yes, sir. That is my axe!"

The *Rukkha-thewada* was pleased to meet such an honest man. "Here, woodcutter. You may take all three axes. Your honesty pleases me."

The woodcutter hurried home with a golden axe, a silver axe, and his own battered metal axe!

Soon news of the poor woodcutter's fortunate encounter with the *Rukkha-thewada* spread throughout the village. His neighbor came over to admire the valuable gold and silver axes. He felt envy. He too wanted to own a gold axe and silver axe.

The next day, this jealous neighbor went into the forest. Instead of cutting and gathering firewood, the neighbor went straight to the river bank and threw his old axe into the river. Then he sat down and prayed to *Rukkha-thewada*. Sure enough, *Rukkha-thewada* appeared before him holding a golden axe in his hand. "Is this your axe?" asked the *Rukkha-thewada*.

The neighbor looked at the golden axe glistening in the sun. How wonderful to own such a lovely and valuable axe. He greedily nodded his head and said, "Yes, sir. That is my axe."

The *Rukkha-thewada* was not pleased with this answer. This man was lying. This was not an honest man. The *Rukkha-thewada* reprimanded the neighbor: "You are telling a lie. I see that you do not follow the Lord Buddha's Five Precepts for Laymen. The Lord

Buddha has taught us: Do not kill any living things. Do not steal. Do not act unchastely. Do not lie. Do not drink intoxicating beverages. *You* have just told me a lie. You do not deserve help from me. Go and find your axe yourself."

The *Rukkha-thewada* disappeared, leaving the neighbor by himself on the riverbank, without his lost axe.

The Thieving Crow

Ungratefulness is considered very poor behavior in Thai life. One should always show proper gratitude to those who provide help. And, of course, the crow's thievery in this tale is totally unacceptable in any case, as one of the Five Buddhist Precepts is "Do not steal."

A crow and a dove were friends. They lived under the kitchen roof of a wealthy man's home. From that spot they flew out every morning to search for food. In the evening the two birds returned home to their nests under the kitchen eaves. The cook in the rich man's house observed the two birds flying in and out. But they did no harm, so he did not disturb their nests.

One day, the crow noticed a heap of raw meat in the kitchen. He couldn't get the thought of that food out of his mind. When he and the dove were some way from their home, the crow said, "Dear Friend, let us go different ways today. You search for food in one direction. I will look in another."

"Don't you think it is better to stay together?" asked the dove. "Remember the old motto: 'Alone you may lose your head. Friends survive united.'"

But the crow replied, "We may find more food by going our separate ways. This way we can cover more ground. Let us try it today."

As soon as the dove had flown off in one direction, the crow turned and flew back to the kitchen where he had seen the meat. Watching his chance, he snatched a piece and flew into his nest to enjoy it in leisure. When that piece was finished, he simply dived down into the kitchen and stole another and another.

When the dove returned, he saw the pile of meat in the crow's nest. "You must have found a large carcass of a buffalo today. How fortunate." Then, looking carefully at the meat, he wondered. "I hope you didn't steal meat from the villagers. Taking their leftovers is always enough to satisfy our hunger. We do not need to steal."

"But wouldn't you steal if you had the chance?" asked the crow. "If it was easy, and you could get away with it? Wouldn't you want to steal then?"

The dove shook his head. "No. I would not steal. I try to find my own food every day, just enough to keep me from hunger. I do not want to take the food which other people need for *their* hunger."

While they were talking, the cook and the servants came into the kitchen. Suddenly one of the servants cried out: "The meat! It has been stolen! Who has done this?"

The dove heard this outcry below in the kitchen. He realized what had happened. "Dear Friend, you must not steal. Such greed will kill you. This cook has been kind to us. The people in this house allow us to live under their roof. They do not harm us. We should be grateful for their generosity. This stealing is an ungrateful act."

The crow turned his head away and did not answer.

Next day, the dove insisted that the crow accompany him in his search for food, but the crow refused. When the dove had flown away, the crow perched where he could see into the kitchen window and watched to see what was good to eat today. Soon the cook brought in a large piece of meat and laid it on the cutting board. The crow waited until the cook walked from the kitchen, then he flew down and began to peck at the hunk of meat. But the meat was so heavy that the crow could not fly with it. Pecking and pulling, pecking and pulling, he struggled with the meat. He did not see the cook come back into the room, pull his cutting knife from his belt, and take aim at the thieving crow. In a moment, the crow was lying dead. Killed by the cook's sharp knife.

The cook picked up the crow's body and tossed it out onto the rubbish pile.

That evening when the dove returned, he saw his friend's body on the ground. He wept and said: "Dear Friend, I reminded you of the right way to live. But you did not follow my well-meaning advice. Now it is too late to save your life."

Chapter 5

Nithan Son Khati Tam: Tales to Make You Think

(or *Nithan Ing Tamma*: Tales to Lead You Toward *Dharma*)

Who Is Best?

In this tale, the three main characters represent three basic Buddhist values: *boon* (boon), *man* (mun), and *panya* (pän-yä). *Boon* refers to merit, which may be gained by having a generous heart, being kind, friendly, and sympathetic to others. *Man* is diligence, the trait of pursuing an end industriously. The *panya*, wisdom, of this story refers to an intuitive wisdom, an insightful knowledge of what is right. Buddhist teaching emphasizes the accumulation of merit through beneficial acts, such as the offering of food to monks, repairing or beautifying the temple, avoiding anti-social behavior, and working to preserve harmonious personal relationships. To become a monk, or "take the saffron robe," even for a short period of time, sends merit to one's parents. Accumulating merit aids one's progress upward in the path toward enlightenment, and, hopefully, results in rebirth on a higher plane.

A long time ago, there were three men who were close friends. The first was named Boon (Merit), the second was named Man (Diligence) and the third was named Panya (Wisdom). Once, during a time of famine, the three men decided to leave for another town to look for jobs. At last, they found a rich farmer who would hire them to clear land for more rice fields. The rich farmer had only one condition. They must finish the task in seven days.

Every morning, a servant brought the three men food for the day. Every evening, the rich farmer came to see how much they had accomplished. The rich farmer was pleased to see that the three men worked very hard. They would be able to accomplish this task within the seven days.

On the last day, the three finished their work early, but nobody brought them their food. They waited and waited, still the servant did not come. While they waited they began to boast among themselves about their names. "My name is the best," said Mr. Boon. "If you lack *boon* (merit) you will not become rich and prosperous even if you are diligent and clever."

Mr. Man interrupted, "No, *my* name is best. Even if you have *boon*, if you do not have *man* (diligence) you will starve to death."

But Mr. Panya disagreed. "No. Even if you have *boon* and *man* you cannot prosper unless you have *panya* (wisdom)."

Suddenly, the three were attacked by hunger. Panya got up and walked around looking for something to eat. He soon noticed a trail of ants. Each ant was carrying a single grain of rice. Right away, he realized that the rich man had sent the food, but that the servant had been instructed to hide it from them. He told his friend Man, "The servant did bring the food. It is hidden. Look for it."

Mr. Man got up and looked around. He searched diligently until he discovered the packet of food, wrapped in its banana leaf covering, hidden in the forest. He brought back the food and shared it with his friend Panya, saying, "If Boon is truly blessed by his previous good deeds and merits, he will have somebody bring him food. He will not need this."

After Panya and Man were full, there was still a bit of food left. So Panya and Man tossed it to Boon. Boon accepted the food gratefully and ate hungrily. But as he finished the food, Boon discovered several pieces of gold in the bottom of the packet! The rich farmer had hidden their promised reward under the food.

Boon was delighted. He showed the money to his friends, who promptly asked for their shares.

Panya said, "If it had not been for my wisdom, we would not have known the food was hidden."

Man said, "If it had not been for my diligence, we would not have found the hidden food."

Boon said, "You two still lack *boon*. Good deeds bring good in return. As you lack merit, you threw your gold away with the food scraps. You cannot say that this gold belongs to you. What is thrown away is no longer yours."

While the three quarreled, the rich farmer arrived. The three asked the rich farmer to be the judge. After hearing their story, the rich man took the six gold pieces and divided them equally among the three. He explained, "Each of you is equally important. No one alone is sufficient. All three are needed. In order to succeed and prosper, a man must have all three of your qualities: merit, diligence, and wisdom."

The Pious Son-in-Law

This tale reminds us of the inexorable law of all existence, impermanence. In Buddhist philosophy, all is in an eternal flux of being, with no beginning and no end. Existence has three characteristics: *Anitchung* (anitjung), or impermanence, *thuk-kang* (too-khung), or conflict, and *anatta* (änättä), or non-self.

Thid Kham's (Tid Khum) title, "Thid," is used for one who has entered monkhood and is therefore considered a fully matured man. His time in the monkhood may be for seven days, a month, or longer. Thid Kham's saying *"Dai dai nai lok luan anitchung"* (Dai dai nai lok loo-an änitjung) could be translated literally as "All conditional things in this world are transient."

Thid Kham was a cautious man. He had, after all, been a monk for 10 years. He was still careful in his actions. He was careful whenever he spoke. Thid Kham was fond of saying *"Dai dai nai lok luan anitchung.* Nothing is certain; all things must pass."

After Thid Kham left the monkhood, he lived as a bachelor for some time, but at last he did fall in love and marry. To everyone's surprise, the pious Thid Kham wed the daughter of the richest man in the village. His new father-in-law, Nai Dee, was a most unholy man. Nai Dee had never even served as a novice, let alone dedicated time to the priesthood. In fact, Nai Dee paid little attention to Buddhist teachings at all. He thought mainly of making money. And then of making more money. Thid Kham's cautiousness did not please him. Nor did Thid Kham's general attitude toward life. Still, Nai Dee loved his daughter, so he tolerated Thid Kham for her sake.

Nai Dee's rice fields covered hundreds of acres. One day, he asked Thid Kham to accompany him on a tour of his fields. As it had been a good year, the fields appeared bountiful. The green rice seedlings stretched to the horizon in every direction. Nai Dee couldn't help bragging. "What do you think, Thid Kham? The fields are growing so well this year that we will sell even more rice than last year!"

But Thid Kham remained cautious. "Father-in-law, this is not certain yet. Even though the rice grows well at the moment, it could be spoiled by a flood before it matures. Our Lord Buddha always reminds us, *'Dai dai nai lok luan anitchung. Nothing is certain; all things must pass.'"*

Nai Dee was not pleased with this answer, but he tried not to show his annoyance. Two months later the rice bloomed. The plants looked remarkably healthy. Again Nai Dee took Thid Kham to the fields. "Thid Kham, see how healthy our rice plants are. They are all bearing blooms. This will surely be a good year for us."

Thid Kham looked around. He answered cautiously. "Father-in-law nothing is certain at this time. Before the harvest, the rice could yet be attacked by insects or mice. Remember our Lord Buddha said, *'Dai dai nai lok luan anitchung. Nothing is certain; all things must pass.'"*

Nai Dee was annoyed. But he did not retort.

When the rice had at last been harvested and put into the granaries, Nai Dee called his son-in-law again. "Thid Kham, look at this. As I said, we have a better harvest than ever before. We are going to be rich."

Thid Kham remained quiet for a moment, then he said thoughtfully, "Father-in-law, nothing is certain in this world. The rice has been harvested and is in the granaries. Still, fire could destroy it before it is sold. As the Lord Buddha has said, *'Dai dai nai lok luan anitchung. Nothing is certain; all things must pass.'"*

Nai Dee had tried to convince Thid Kham, but without success. He told his servants to cook some of the rice and prepare it for their meal. On the table stood bowls of the steaming, freshly cooked rice. Nai Dee offered a bowl to his son-in-law and watched as Thid Kham lifted the rice to his mouth. Nai Dee tried one last time to make his stubborn son-in-law change his philosophy.

"Thid Kham, what do you say now about this rice? Isn't this certain? It ripened, it was harvested, it was stored, it was cooked, and it goes into your mouth. Is this not now a certain thing?"

Thid Kham looked at his father-in-law's impatient face. But he answered with respect. "No, Father-in-law, nothing is certain. As the Lord Buddha says, '*Dai dai nai lok luan anitchung*. Nothing is certain; all things must pass.'"

As Thid Kham uttered these words, his enraged father-in-law shot out his hand and knocked the rice bowl from Thid Kham's mouth. "If nothing is certain, then leave my table! You will insist forever on this foolish philosophy!"

Thid Kham rose slowly, brushing the spilled rice from his clothing. "Father-in-law, nothing is certain. Everyone here can see what has happened. The rice ripened, it was harvested, it was stored, it was cooked. The rice grains touched my mouth, and yet they were lost to me. Is it not clear, Father-in-law? Nothing is certain; all things must pass."

Nai Dee nodded slowly. "It is true. My Son-in-Law, it is true. *Dai dai nai lok luan anitchung*. Nothing is certain; all things must pass."

He Who Thinks He Is First Is Unwise

To be humble is a valued character trait in Thailand. One learns from a very young age not to be boastful, to downplay the self, even to carefully control one's body movements so as not to attract attention or impose on another's space. Since Thai culture calls for modesty, bragging or putting oneself ahead of others is improper. This tale notes the folly of thinking you are number one.

Once, long ago, there lived a very proud *phraya* (prayä) or lord. This Thai officer had been given the title by the king. This particular *phraya* had an extremely large sword. It was two feet wide and four meters long! Every day the *phraya* sharpened his sword. He would test the blade and boast to his wife, "Dear Wife, my sword is so sharp that it could slice two buffalo in half just as easily as cutting through a banana tree."

Every day Phraya sharpened his sword and made the same boast to his wife. After a while, she became so irritated with his bragging ways that she spoke to him. "Dear Husband, do not think that you are better than others. Look at that tall tree there. To us it seems the tallest tree in the forest, but there will be taller trees somewhere."

Phraya was not pleased to hear his wife suggest that there might be someone somewhere who was better than he. He shouted at her. "If you think there is another man somewhere better than I, I will go and look for him. But if I do not find such a person, have caution, Dear Wife, for I will come back here and slice off your head with this very sword!"

The wife was not afraid. She was too angry with her husband's foolishness to have second thoughts. She challenged him, "Yes, go ahead. If this is what you will do, then *do* it. If I am wrong, you can come back and behead me with your treacherous sword!"

Phraya was furious. He felt his wife had slighted him. He intended to prove to her that what she said was wrong. He, Phraya, with his wonderful sword, was the best man, better than any other man in the world!

He left his house and wandered from town to town. He assumed he would not find anyone better than himself. Still, he searched.

One day, Phraya was walking along a rice field in the hot noon sun. He saw some children emptying water out of a small pond. As soon as it was drained they would be able to catch fish in the muddy bottom. The children were sweating profusely with their efforts in that heat.

Suddenly, one of the children stopped. "It is too hot to work under this sun. Why don't we move the pond into the shade?" The other children agreed. While Phraya watched, those small children picked up the pond and carried it over into a shady area under the trees. "How did they do that?" he wondered.

But when he approached the children, and questioned them about this marvel, they merely shook their heads. "Dear Phraya, this is such a simple task. We cannot presume to teach you such a simple thing. There are many others who know much more than we do. We are children and know but little. There are people much better than us who could advise you."

Phraya remembered that his wife had also said something similar to that. Still, he did not want to accept that his wife might be right. He decided to search further.

One day, just at noontime, Phraya passed a field where a Buddhist novice was cutting tall grass. The sun was very hot. "It is lunch time. Let's take a break from this hot work," said the Buddhist novice to his helpers. Then he and all of his helpers opened their banana leaf lunch packets. Each of them sat down gently with legs crossed on *top* of the tall grass! Yet not one blade of grass bent. Not one of the workers fell to the ground.

Phraya was amazed. "Here is another thing about which I know nothing!" he thought. Phraya approached the Buddhist novice. "Please tell me how you accomplish this feat." But the

Buddhist novice declined, "Dear Phraya, why do you ask about this. This is just a simple trick. I know little as yet. There are many men who know much more than I. It is they who should teach you."

Again, Phraya remembered the words that his wife had spoken. Still, he was too stubborn to give up. He continued his journey.

One day, he reached a town just as night fell. Phraya was tired and wanted to pause and smoke for a while. He took his cigar from his pocket, but could not find a match. Seeing a man working in a nearby rice field, Phraya approached him. But when he drew closer, he realized that this man was really an *artificial* man. This town was so advanced that they employed mechanical men to do their work instead of humans.

Phraya was intrigued. "Here again is something about which I know nothing!" Phraya went to the owner of the mechanical man. "Please, teach me to construct an artifical man like this!" But the farmer who owned the mechanical man just shook his head, "Dear Phraya, building an artifical worker like this is such an easy task. I could not presume to be your teacher. I know but little. There are many who are much wiser and more knowledgable than I. It is they who should be your teacher. There are men who are much better than I!"

Phraya knew he had heard that phrase before. Still, he did not want to accept the possibility that he might be wrong. He walked on.

At last, he reached the ocean. On the beach, a man was fishing. That fisherman was using a live elephant as bait! He threw his rod into the water and caught a fish with his bait. That fish was three acres across! Phraya had been traveling for so long that he was starved. He missed the good cooking of his wife. Phraya asked the fisherman, "Dear Fisherman, may I have a little piece of your fish to eat for my dinner?"

The fisherman welcomed him. "Of course, Phraya. Help yourself. Take as much as you want. Why don't you use your sword and cut off a piece of this fish?"

He Who Thinks He Is First Is Unwise

Phraya took his precious sword out of its cover. He attempted to filet a piece from the huge fish. His sword was so big it would not cut into that fish. All morning he hacked away. All evening he tried to cut that fish. Without success.

Late that night, the fisherman returned and saw that Phraya still had not cut any meat from the fish. He took Phraya's sword and examined it. He touched it's blade, then made a face. "Phraya why do you use such a big and useless sword? It cannot cut anything at all!" The fisherman removed a small knife from his bag. "Here Phraya. Try a filet knife."

Phraya took the knife and sliced the fish. He watched as the small knife cut easily through the fish. As Phraya ate his fish, he thought.

Phraya had been a fool. He had been a pompous and stubborn man. It was time to return to his home. Phraya found his wife at his door waiting for him. As soon as she saw Phraya's face, the wife knew she had been right. "Wife, you were right," said Phraya. "There are many people in this world who are wiser than I am. I am not better than everyone after all. From now on, I will learn to be more humble." And that is just what Phraya did.

Plenty

In Thai culture, it is believed that people should work out their differences and learn to get along together. In this story, even a small child can show the arguing married couple the error of their ways. They are tripped up by that despised trait, greed.

Once there was a couple who lived together for a very long time. They became wealthy and had several children together. But eventually, they quarreled and decided to separate. They decided that, as they had been without property when they married, everything they had should be divided equally. There was no problem dividing their money, their rice fields, their houses, and their children. But they could not agree on how to divide their rice. Each wanted *"nak kae"* (nak-ke), "plenty" of rice. The judge could not decide just how much was *"nak kae."*

The judge took the case to the king, but the king and his court could not decide either. How much was *"nak kae?"* No matter what anyone suggested, the old couple was not satisfied with the division.

As the story was told throughout the town, a young boy heard the tale. He went to the king. "I can divide the rice for this couple in such a way that they will both be satisfied." The king agreed to let the young boy try. The old couple was brought to the court to hear the boy's verdict.

When the couple had arrived, the boy asked for all the rice in question to be piled in the middle of the room. Then he asked of the husband, "How much rice do you want?" "Nak kae. Plenty!" was the reply. He asked the wife the same question. "Nak kae. Plenty!" "Very well," said the boy, "I will let each of you have 'nak kae' rice."

Both husband and wife were delighted. The boy continued speaking. "You may each use this small bamboo container to carry your rice. You, husband, pile your rice over here at this end of the yard. You, wife, pile your rice over there at that end. You may take only one container full of rice at a time. But you may take as much rice as you please."

The couple was pleased with this decision. They believed that it was a just decision. Each felt certain of getting *nak kae* rice.

The young boy cried "Begin!" and both husband and wife hurriedly dug into the rice pile with their small containers. Each ran to deposit the rice at the end of the yard. The quicker they ran, the more rice they got. They dipped, carried, and ran. Dipped, carried, and ran. At last they were exhausted and could not move anymore. They stopped, huffed, and sat down by the rice pile. The young boy asked, "Do you have *nak kae* rice now?" They nodded their heads in exhaustion. Breathing heavily they sighed "*Nak kae, nak kae!*"

"So," said the boy, "if you have *nak kae* now, that is your share of the rice. The rest of the pile belongs to the king." Everyone who heard of this decision was pleased with it. They praised the young boy's wisdom everywhere.

The Good Boy

To be respectful of elders is a valued character trait in Thailand. One should always pay respect to one's elders, either in age or in status. One usually calls all elders by a respectful title such as Uncle, *Lung* (Loong) or Aunt, *Pa* (Pä) , or Grandfather, *Ta* (Tä) or Grandmother, *Yai* (Yäi) even though they are not actually relatives.

In Thailand, in the olden days, elephants played an important role in life. Elephants were used as trucks and tractors in forestry. They pulled logs from high mountains, dragging them down to the river banks. Elephants were also used as fighting tanks in war. Wild elephants were rounded up and brought to a training school, where they were trained to be either working elephants or fighting elephants. Albino elephants or "white elephants" were considered rare and sacred. Any king who owned a white elephant was considered great. Today, elephants are still used in the timber industry in Northern Thailand.

Once there was a boy whose parents were very poor. Still, they were good parents. They taught the boy to be obedient and considerate. They taught him to be respectful of all elders, regardless of their social status or wealth. This child was a good boy. He followed the ways his parents had taught him.

One day, when the boy was searching for wood in the forest, he became lost. He felt very frightened, but he tried to look for signs which might show him the way back to his home. As he searched this way and that, the boy suddenly came face to face with a huge, full-grown elephant that was strolling through the forest munching on bamboo and wild bananas. The boy was terrified at the sight of this huge animal, but he remembered his parents' admonitions to respect great age. This elephant was so large that it must be very old indeed. Trembling, the boy knelt and bowed three times in respect to the great elephant.

Seeing this, the elephant was surprised. He came closer to the boy and asked, "Young boy, why do you show respect to me?"

The boy answered, "Dear Elephant the Mighty One, I bow down because you are strong. I bow down because you are my elder. My parents taught me to pay respect to all who deserve respect. I believe you are one of those, therefore I pay homage to you."

"You are a good boy," said the elephant. "You follow your elders' instructions. I will reward your good conduct. This bell was given to me by the King of the Elephants. I now give it to you. If ever you are in danger or in need of help, you should ring this bell. Any elephants who are nearby will come at once to your rescue."

The boy gratefully accepted the bell. He thanked the elephant. Then the elephant showed the boy the way back to his village. "Follow this path and it will lead to your home. I must leave you now." The elephant turned, and disappeared into the deep forest.

The boy followed the elephant's advice and soon reached his home. He told his parents about the encounter with the elephant. They were pleased that their son had received this gift from the elephant. All this because he was such a good boy, doing exactly what his parents had taught him.

Several months later, the boy and his father went back into the forest to gather firewood. They planned to make charcoal to sell on New Year's Day. They left home early in the morning and the father worked to cut branches from a large tree. Suddenly, a storm came up. The boy and his father took refuge in the crevice of a large rock, but the tree on which the father had been cutting broke in half in the wind. The tree fell right across the crevice, trapping the boy and his father. They were unhurt, but unable to escape. They called for help, but so deep in the forest, there was no one to hear.

For several hours, they huddled in the rock crevice, then the boy remembered his gift, the elephant bell. He pulled out the bell and began to ring it. Soon the boy and his father heard a crashing sound, as several elephants came lumbering through the forest.

Wrapping their strong trunks around the tree, the elephants lifted it from the rock and the trapped boy and his father were freed. Gratefully, the boy bowed before the elephants and thanked them. It was as his friend, the elephant, had said. Help had come immediately.

Meanwhile his elephant friend had fallen on bad luck. He had been captured and imprisoned in the city where he was being trained as a fighting elephant. His huge size made him a fierce fighter, but his wild temperament did not allow him to adapt to this life. Eventually, he went mad. The wild elephant killed his trainers and escaped into the jungle. From there he would emerge, raging, to devastate villages. Elephant trainers were sent to capture him, but they returned injured and the elephant's reign of terror continued.

When the boy heard of this wild elephant, he volunteered at once to try to capture it. His parents begged him not to undertake such a dangerous task, but the boy showed them his bell, and assured them that this bell would help him accomplish the risky mission.

The boy hurried to the king's palace and volunteered his services. The king's soldiers escorted the boy to the area where the wild elephant was currently raging, but as soon as the elephant emerged from the forest, those soldiers ran for their lives, leaving the boy standing alone.

The elephant bellowed and prepared to attack. The boy calmly spread a cloth on the ground. There, he bowed three times to the enraged beast, ringing his bell all the while.

Suddenly, the elephant stopped. It heard the bell and it remembered. The elephant walked slowly to the boy and laid its trunk on top of the boy's head to greet him.

Talking softly to the elephant, the boy reassured it. He persuaded it to go back to town with him. and the huge elephant calmly walked beside the boy, back to the king's palace.

The king was very pleased. He rewarded the boy and appointed him head of the elephant troop. This boy was a good boy. With this excellent job, he took fine care of his parents when they grew old.

The Good Boy

Medicine to Revive the Dead

Acceptance of whatever life brings is important in Thai thought. Acceptance of death is brought about by reminding oneself *"Anitchung watta sangkhara"* (Äni-tjung wät-tä säng-khä-rä), which means "impermanent and changing are all things." Life and death are seen as a constantly revolving wheel.

This story of Lady Kisa's meeting with the Buddha is well known throughout Southeast Asia. When death comes, one remembers this story. The story helps one to realize that death must be accepted as a part of life.

Once long ago, the Lord Buddha was staying at Chetawan Garden in Sawathee City. While he was there, the Lady Kisa Khotami's only baby died. Lady Kisa was near to losing her mind with sorrow at the loss of her child. She could not stop crying. This had been her only son. He had been just at that cute and cuddly age when babies are so loveable. How could such an innocent baby die? So young. With such a long future ahead of him.

Kisa refused to accept that her only child could die. She would not cremate him. She would not let anyone come close to touch her son's dead body. Hugging him close to her bosom, she walked from house to house, from door to door, asking if anyone could help bring her son back to life. The physicians shook their heads in pity. This baby was beyond help. This baby was dead.

The villagers all felt sorry for Lady Kisa, but nobody could revive the baby. At last someone suggested that Kisa should go to see the Lord Buddha.

With her hope's raised, Kisa hurriedly walked to Chetawan Garden. There the Lord Buddha was giving a sermon to his followers. With tear-covered face, Kisa moved close to Buddha. She held out the tiny dead body to Buddha and begged, "Please,

Our Lord Buddha. Please help revive my baby. Please bring his life back to me. I beg you with all my heart, Sir."

"Dear Kisa," answered Lord Buddha, with eyes full of pity, "if you can find me some cabbage seeds from a house where nobody ever dies, I will make a medicine to revive your child."

Kisa was elated. Finally, she had found a way to bring her son back to life. She determined that she would go to the end of the world if need be to find whatever was needed for this magic medicine that would revive her dead baby.

Kisa ran out of the garden. She ran all the way back to the village. Kisa knocked on door after door. Did anyone have cabbage seeds? Yes, most households had some cabbage seeds which they would give her. "Has anyone in this house ever died?" At each household someone nodded. "My grandfather ... just last month." "My son ... two years ago." "My mother...."

Kisa did not give up. She searched every house in the village, asking her question. At each house she received the same answer. Again and again she heard of death. She searched and searched. She walked and walked. From morning to evening she continued. At last she was exhausted. Still, she had not found a house in which nobody had ever died. Depressed and disappointed, Kisa returned to Lord Buddha.

Then Lord Buddha spoke to her. "Kisa listen to what I have to say. Here is the truth of life. Death is natural. Once there is a birth, there must follow a death. Everybody who is born must die. There is no exception to this. Men, animals, plants, all must die. The only variable is time. Some may die sooner than others. If one does not die while young, one will die when one is old. If one does not die peacefully, one will die painfully. No exception. Kings, the rich, the poor, the gods, Brahman, Indra, even the monks who try to avoid sin, all will die when the time has come."

Kisa listened carefully to what the Lord Buddha said. Finally she saw the truth. Yes, those who were born must die. If not sooner, later. Rich or poor. Beautiful or ugly. All would die some day. Nobody could avoid death. It was nature's way. One had to accept the inevitable as gracefully as one could.

Once she realized this fact of life, according to Buddha's teaching, peace came to Kisa's mind. She no longer felt distraught. She agreed to cremate her son's dead body. It was this Kisa who later became one of Buddha's most faithful disciples.

When Death Comes

Buddhist beliefs counsel people to exercise free will. One should try to develop an indifferent attitude toward emotions—whether sorrow, disappointment, anger, or irritation—with an understanding that whatever happens, happens according to karmic forces and must therefore be accepted without moroseness.

One freely chooses to improve his future by doing good deeds, making merits. Life and death to the Buddhist are but two opposites of the same cyclical existence. The Thai Buddhist strives to develop *plongtok* (plongtok), the state of controlling one's own mind, being indifferent to whatever befalls, and accepting whatever happens with mindfulness but without sadness.

It is customary in many Asian countries to cremate the body of a dead person, burning, rather than burying, is seen as the proper way to return the human body to the elements.

There once was a family of six who lived together in a small hut. They were father, mother, son, daughter, daughter-in-law, and a maid.

One day, father and son went to the rice field to plough the land. It was hot, and they worked hard. Then, as the son was plowing, he stepped on a cobra and was bitten by the snake. He fell to the ground and he died. Though the father was with the son, there was nothing he could do. Everything had happened so fast. One minute, the son was alive, working in the field. Then, suddenly, he was bitten, fallen, and lying dead.

When he realized that there was nothing he could do to save his son's life, the father carried the dead body to the shade of a large tree. Laying the body carefully in the tree's shade, the father turned and went back to his work in the field.

At noon, he saw a neighbor going home for lunch. "Neighbor, please tell my wife at home to bring only one lunch today. She does not need to bring a lunch for my son this day. But ask her to tell everyone in our home to come here at once. Thank you, Neighbor."

The neighbor told the wife what the father had asked. When his family had gathered around him in the field, the father told them of the thing which had befallen the son. No one in this family cried. Silently, they began to gather firewood for a crematory fire. Silently, they built the fire. Silently, they laid the son's body onto the burning pyre. Silently, they watched the son's body as it was reduced to ashes.

At that moment, a Brahman was passing by. He saw the family gathered quietly around the burning ashes. "Who are you cremating?" he asked. "It is my son, Dear Brahman. We are his family. Here is his mother, his wife, his sister, and his maid."

The Brahman was surprised to see that none of the son's family wept or seemed in distress. "I beg your pardon, Dear Farmer. Is this really your son who has died?"

"Yes. This was my son. He was bitten this morning by a cobra. It happened right here in the rice field in front of my eyes."

"But Dear Farmer, why do you not look sad? Your son must have been really bad. You do not even cry for him."

The farmer said, "No, it is not so. My son was a very obedient child. He respected his elders. He was a good man. But this is as it is with the snake. Once the snake sheds its skin, it does not think about that old skin any more. If somebody tramples the skin, the snake does not get angry; it does not worry; it does not become sad. It is the same with my son's death. If I burn his body, he will not become angry or sad that I have destroyed that body. This, to me, is truth. Therefore, I am not sad that my son is dead.

The Brahman nodded his head in agreement. Then he turned to the mother. "But surely you would cry for your son's death if you love him at all?"

The Mother answered, "I, like all mothers, love my son dearly. Still, when my son entered my womb, he did not forewarn me of his coming. Nor did I invite him. He just came. I loved him and raised him. I taught him to be a good citizen. Now that it was time for my son to leave, he did not say goodbye. Nor did I ask him to go. He just left. If I cried he would not know. And my tears would not help him. This, to me, is truth. Therefore I do not cry."

The Brahman turned to the wife, "You and your husband must have quarreled often, because you do not even cry for him." The wife of the dead son answered. "Dear Brahman, my husband was a faithful and loving husband. I do love him very much, but a child, who understands nothing, may cry for the moon in the sky. Yet the child will never get that moon. My husband has just died. If I cried until my tears turned to blood, still this would not bring back my husband's life. This I understand. This, to me, is truth. I do not cry."

"But you, his sister, do you not grieve for your brother? Was he so cruel that you do not mourn his passing?"

The Sister addressed the Brahman. "Dear Brahman, my brother was a good brother to me. But when a needle falls into the ocean, it is impossible to retrieve it. This is the same as my brother's life. His life is now lost. Though I cried until my body dropped from exhaustion, I still could not retrieve his lost life. I will never find that needle lost in the ocean again. Nor will I ever see my brother alive again. The cobra's poison has certainly killed my brother. This, to me, is truth. Therefore, I do not cry."

To the maid he said, "You do not mourn this young man? He must have treated you cruelly."

The maid said, "My Respectable Brahman. This young man treated me very well. Once a rice pot breaks, we feel sorry. We want the pot back in its original shape. We cry until our eyes become blind. And yet that pot does not become whole again. It is the same with our tears for the dead. No amount of crying will bring the dead back to life. This, to me, is truth. Therefore I do not cry for the dead."

Once the Brahman, that learned man, understood the logic of this farmer and his family, he praised them. He applauded their clear thinking and their ability to accept death calmly and reasonably.

If It Belongs to Us, It Will Come to Us

The Thai believe one should accept whatever life brings gracefully. The things which come to one in this life are the result of good or bad deeds one has performed in past lives. Therefore you are only receiving what you deserve, what your past actions have earned. This is the *karma* you have created for yourself. You should accept it. Of course, your future *karma* depends on your actions in *this* life. So you should try to do good deeds now to improve your *karma*.

There once was an old man and an old woman who lived in a hut near a rice field. This was a hardworking couple. But, even though they worked hard all day long, they were very poor. They worked hard in their field. They foraged in the forest for plants, herbs, and firewood to sell. Still they remained poor.

One day, while the couple were clearing away a termite mound in the rice field, the old man struck something hard with his hoe. He dug the object up and found it to be a huge jar. How strange. Inside the jar was a great quantity of gold! The jar was *filled* with gold. The old man called to his wife.

The old woman in "If It Belongs to Us, It Will Come to Us" might have looked like the woman in this photograph.

"Old Woman, come quickly! Someone has hidden a jar of gold in our rice field." His wife hurried over and helped clear the dirt from around the jar. It was filled to the brim with gold. The wife was delighted.

"Old Man, find something to carry this gold home!"

The old man shook his head.

"Dear Old Woman, I do not think that is a good idea. This gold does not belong to us. We should leave it here."

The old woman argued with the old man. But he spoke calmly to her. "Old Woman, if it belongs to us, it will come to us. We cannot take what is not clearly ours."

Reluctlantly the old woman agreed. She tried to convince the old man to change his mind on this matter, but he remained firm.

When they arrived home, the old woman told her neighbors about their find. They just laughed at her. Nobody believed her words. But one day some passing buffalo traders heard the story. They found the termite mound and dug up the jar. Gingerly they opened it, then jumped back in alarm. "What a lie!" In the huge jar they found, not gold, but a huge snake, lying coiled inside, filling the jar with its body. "They can't get away with telling us such a lie. Let's teach that old couple a lesson."

Finding a strong liana vine from the forest, they tied it around the jar and pulled it onto their wagon. Late that night, they dropped the jar right in front of the old couple's hut. They turned the jar onto its side, removed the cover, and nudged open the old couple's door. Then they hurried away into the night, certain that the snake would enter the house and strike the old couple.

The next morning, the old woman got up before dawn as usual to prepare their breakfast. It was still dark when she pushed open the door and stepped outside. She stumbled over the huge jar and gave a cry of fright. Her husband jumped from his sleeping mat and ran to see what had happened. There was the huge jar from the field, lying on its side right in front of their door.

"Who could have brought this to our door? Who would have done such a thing?" The old man was puzzled. He brought a candle and they inspected the jar. It was filled with gold.

Nithan Son Khati Tam: **Tales to Make You Think**

"Is this really gold?" gasped the old woman. "Husband, does this mean the gold is ours?"

"Yes," the old man agreed. "It is as I said. 'If it belongs to us, it will come to us.' It has come. So it must be ours."

The old woman nodded solemnly. "Yes dear. I see now that it is just as you have said. 'If it belongs to us, it will come to us.'"

Color Plates

Ph.1. Huge trees like those cut by Lung Ta, the Woodcutter. (See page 1)

Ph.2. This elephant helps loggers drag trees from the forest. He is taking a break and has put grass on his head to cool himself down.

Ph.11. Two young boys "put on the saffron robe" to become Buddhist novices for the day at their grandfather's funeral. This act of making merit will help the dead grandfather toward a higher rebirth.

Ph.12. Southern Thai shadow puppets—an orgress confronts a tiger.

Ph.13. Traditional Thai musicians. The instruments from left to right are Ja-kae (on floor, performer not visible); Saw-au (played with a bow), Ranat-ek (played with mallets); Saw-duang (played with a bow); Ranat-thump (on floor, not being played), Klui (flute), ching (small cymbals), and Khim.

Ph.14. Seattle, Washington's "Siam Sangkit" dancers wear brightly colored Thai silk dresses interwoven with golden threads for brilliance. The dress consists of a pasin (wraparound skirt), a pleated sabai (scarf wound around and around the bodice), and a gold threaded sabai thrown over the shoulder.

Ph.15. Charie Vathanaprida performs the "Manora." She represents the Bird Maiden, Manora, from a popular Thai folktale.

Ph.16. Performing the "Rabam Dok Bua" (The Dance of the Lotus Flowers).

Chapter 6

Tamnan: Local Legends

Muang Laplae: The Land of Fantasy

The magical land of *Muang Laplae* (Mooung Läp-le) is well-known in Thai folklore. It is sometimes called "The Land of the Widows," because the husbands brought there by beautiful girls always ended up breaking the taboos of that magical land and being banished forever from their wives and families. Some locate Muang Laplae at a cave near Phetchaburi (Pétch-a-bur-ee), a town about 165 kilometers southwest of Bangkok. Phetchaburi is well known for its palm groves and delicious sweets made from palm sugar. Others say Muang Laplae is to be found in Uttaradit City (Oot-tra-ra-dit), north of Bangkok.

The *pakhama* (päkhamä) used by the young man in this story is a long cloth, which can be used for a wrap, a sleeping cloth, a turban, or many other uses. The cumin given to him by his wife is a spice, gold in color, used in Thai cooking. *Klap* (klap) is ground up rice husks. After the rice is threshed, the husks are ground into a fine powder, which can be fed to chickens or mixed into pig food.

One of the Buddhist Five Precepts for Laymen is "Do not lie." The young man's lie in this story ends his happiness.

For hundreds of years, this tale has been told and retold in the city of Phetchaburi. Long, long ago, there was nothing in the area around Wat Boonthawi (Wat Boontawe) and Wat Thamklap (Wat Tamklap) but palm trees. There were no houses there, no *wat*, only trees. It was strange that though palm trees grew everywhere in that region, near a certain cave there was a flat area where no trees grew at all. Only ground rice husks, *klap,* lay around the cave entrance. If anyone cleared out the rice husks, by the next day there would be more littered about in the same place. People called that cave "Tham Klap" (Täm Klap), or "Cave of the rice husks." This was a shallow cave, with no exit from the cave's rear.

One day a young man from Phetchaburi came to collect palms from the trees near the cave. He had climbed one of the tall palms and begun his work when he noticed a group of beautiful young girls approaching the cave. They were carrying empty market baskets swinging from the poles on their shoulders. The girls swayed gracefully as they walked beneath his tree. As each young girl reached the cave opening, she touched something to the cave wall and then disappeared into the cave.

The young man was curious. He watched and waited. No one emerged from the cave. Where could those young girls have vanished to? He was certain the cave had no other entrance. Descending from his palm tree, the young man searched the cave inside and out. There was no sign of the beautiful young girls.

The next day, this young man returned to the cave early in the morning. He climbed the palm tree and waited. Soon the young girls emerged from the cave again. This time their baskets were filled with fresh fruit and vegetables. Talking and laughing, they walked off to the market. But as each girl emerged, she stooped and hid something in the rocks by the cave's entrance.

As soon as the girls had gone, the young man came down from his palm tree. He went straight to the cave and examined the girls' hiding place. There was nothing there except a pile of oddly shaped leaves. He picked one up and examined it, then tossed it aside and returned to his work.

Later that evening, he heard the chattering girls returning. Quickly, he hid himself and watched. As each girl arrived with her empty market basket, she picked up a leaf from the hiding place, touched the leaf to the cave wall, and entered. One by one the beautiful girls entered the cave.

But when the last girl reached into the hiding place, she gasped. There was no leaf left! Her leaf was missing! Her friends had vanished into the cave and she could not follow. She sat down and began to weep.

The young man did not hesitate. He came down from his palm tree and went straight to the girl. "Young Maiden, why are you crying? Can I help you in some way?"

Through her tears the girl explained that she was a citizen of Muang Laplae. That fairy land could be reached through this very cave, but only with the use of her magic leaf could she enter. And her leaf was gone.

On hearing this, the young man told her to dry her tears. He looked around on the ground and soon found the leaf he had tossed away. He returned it to the stranded girl. In her delight at finding her precious lost leaf, this girl invited him to come back with her to Muang Laplae. Why not? Taking her hand, he followed her into the cave and into the magical land of Muang Laplae.

Of course once he had entered fairy land, the young man had no care to return to his home again. He fell in love with the young woman he had befriended. They were married. They lived together happily and even had a son.

Now there was one prohibition within the kingdom of Muang Laplae. No one must ever tell a lie. Not for any reason whatsoever.

One day, while his wife went to market in Phetchaburi, the young man remained caring for his son. The child began to cry for his mother. He played with the child, brought it toys, did everything he could, but his son kept crying for his mother. At last, in desperation the father lied to the child. "You can stop crying, your mother is coming back right now. She will be here any minute now."

His mother-in-law was passing just at that moment and heard him say this thing. All of the citizens of Muang Laplae gathered in assembly. There was nothing to do but expel this young man from their kingdom. He had broken their prohibition. He had told a lie.

Muang Laplae: **The Land of Fantasy**

Even his wife could not save him. But before he left, she presented him with a packet of cumin. Cumin is a spice, used to give Thai curries their delicious flavor. It is just the color of gold. "Dear husband, take good care of this cumin. Carry it home with you and look after it."

Then she led him to the gate of the town and bid him farewell. The young man was sorry for his mistakes. He had not meant to tell a lie, and yet it had slipped out. Now it was too late. He had to leave his lovely wife and his child. Sadly, he walked back through the cave and into his own world.

It was a very hot day in the young man's world. As he trudged toward home, he felt weighted down by the huge packet of cumin. Thinking of his bad luck, he became frustrated with his wife. Why had she burdened him with such a heavy package? Of what use would this be to him? Stopping, he tossed most of the cumin away. He kept only one small piece of the cumin, tying it to his *pakhama*.

When the young man reached home, his relatives hurried to see him. They thought he had fallen from a palm tree and died in the forest. They were glad to have him back among them. The young man was so tired and hot from his long trek through the forest that he could hardly talk to them at first. He pulled off his *pakhama* to mop his forehead. Something heavy fell from the *pakhama* and landed on the ground with a thunk. Picking it up, he stopped in wonder. This was a piece of solid gold, in the shape of a cumin root.

He realized at once that he had tossed away the gift of his lovely wife. How much gold he must have had! And now, only one small piece was left. Though the young man retraced his steps and searched everywhere, he never recovered the lost golden cumin roots. And though he visited the cave time and again, never more did he see the beautiful girls from the land of Muang Laplae.

Tamnan: Local Legends

Mouse Island and Cat Island

Many Thai legends have attached themselves to specific places in the land. This legend gives us the origin of Koh Nu (Mouse Island) and Koh Maeo (Cat Island) at Songkla (Songkhlä) in Southern Thailand. Khrut (Khroot), the mythical creature in this story, is the *Garuda* of India. He is a traditional enemy of snakes, fighting constantly with Naga (Näkha), the serpent. The winged Khrut is part man, part bird. Though he is cast as a helper in this story, Khrut is not always so gentle with humans.

The *pakhama* (pä-kha-mä) is a long multi-purpose piece of cloth used by men to wrap around themselves when swimming, for a head covering, a sleeping cloth, whatever is needed (see photograph on page 80). The *pakhama* was very useful in the rural Thai way of life. The *sarong* (sa-rong) is also a piece of cloth wrapped around the body as clothing, but is of finer quality and is not employed for such varied uses as the *pakhama*.

The housewarming ceremony performed here is traditionally performed whenever someone moves into a new house. The monks are invited to bless the home. A sacred cord is extended around the bounds of the property, or a cord is blessed to symbolize these boundaries. Using the *bai mayom* (bai mä-yom) leaf, the monk sprinkles sacred water around the property and onto the homeowners and guests. Food is offered to the monk and the monk gives a blessing to those gathered there.

You will notice that the Chinese are the enemy in this story. The Thai are uncomfortable with their huge Chinese neighbor to the north. It is not surprising that in Thai tales the Chinese are often cast as villains and are tricked or defeated.

These young men wear *pakhama* on their way to bathe at the river, just like the young man in "Mouse Island and Cat Island." Notice the different ways the *pakhama* can be worn.

Once upon a time, on the shores of Songkla, there lived a poor young man who worked at farming. He was honest and generous to everyone. And although he was poor, he was content.

As time passed, the young man's situation did not improve. He was penniless. All he owned was one *sarong* and one old *pakhama* cloth.

Every day, after breakfast, the young man went to work in his vegetable garden. At noon, he returned home for his lunch, then he went back to work again. This was his daily routine.

One day, after his work was finished, the young man picked some vegetables and brought them home with him. As the sun was still very hot during his walk home, he stopped at the pond, put on his *pakhama*, and went for a swim. Refreshed and cool, he climbed out of the pond, wrung out his *pakhama*, spread it out to dry on top of the tall grasses, and changed back into his *sarong*.

Eager to get home, the young man picked up his load of vegetables and hurried off, forgetting his *pakhama*. He cooked his evening meal and enjoyed the fresh vegetables, without a thought for his forgotten *pakhama*.

Khrut (Khrout) is a mythical creature half man, half bird. In Thailand a Khrut flag signifies the King's transport. It is flown on any car, boat, or plane used by the King.

Now that very day, Khrut happened to fly over the pond where the young man had left his *pakhama*. Looking down, Khrut saw the wet *pakhama* lying curled on top of the grasses, looking just like a resting snake. Khrut always attacks snakes when he sees them, so Khrut swept down, snatched the *pakhama*, and flew off with it.

After his evening meal, the young man remembered his *pakhama*. He hurried back to the pond but it was nowhere in sight. He looked everywhere but could not find it. At last he had to give up the search and turn sadly home. He kept thinking about tomorrow. What would he do without his *pakhama*? What would he use for swimwear? Now he had lost the only possession he had, other than the *sarong* he was wearing.

That night, near dawn, a knock came on the door. The young man was curious. Who could be knocking on his door at such an early hour. He opened the door and found, to his surprise, a handsome and well-dressed person. The stranger bowed to the young man and said, "Dear Brother, please excuse me for waking you at this early hour when you should be sleeping comfortably in your bed."

The young man was very polite. He did not show anger with the stranger. But politely he said, "That is all right. You did not bother me at all. It is time to get up anyway." The strange young man came forward and handed the poor man his lost *pakhama*, saying softly, "Yesterday, I was walking past the pond and found this *pakhama*. I did not know that it belonged to you, therefore I took it. Now that I know, I want to return the *pakhama* to you."

Seeing his old *pakhama*, the young man was elated. He accepted it and said, "That's right. It is my *pakhama*. I have to thank you for bringing it back to me. Please come in and have breakfast with me. I will be delighted to have company."

The handsome young stranger could not resist the young man's persistent and sincere invitation. He entered the house and took breakfast with the young man. Looking around at the condition of the house and the food on the table, he was sorry for the poor young man. The whole house was bare. There was no furniture at all. Even so, the poor man was very kind. He loved animals and kept two dogs and one cat as pets. All three pets looked healthy and well-fed. This showed that the young man was kind, even though he was so poor.

Before departing, the handsome stranger took a crystal out of his pocket and gave it to the poor man. He said, "Dear Brother, I want to give you this magic crystal. This crystal can grant you any wish. Please accept it. Now I have to say farewell to you."

The poor man graciously accepted the crystal and said humbly, "Dear Brother, I thank you very much for this gift. All I wish is that my vegetables grow quickly and beautifully."

After the handsome stranger had left, the young man went to tend his vegetable garden. When he reached the garden, he was so surprised that he exclaimed loudly, "Whose garden is *this*? The vegetables look so big and beautiful!"

He looked around to make sure he was in the right place. Yes, this was his very own garden. But the vegetables were wonderfully beautiful, big, and healthy. Thinking back, he remembered what he had said to the handsome stranger. "That must be it! This must be because of the crystal that the handsome stranger gave me."

From that day on, the poor man cut his vegetables and shared them with his neighbors. Word of his generosity and his beautiful vegetables spread through the whole village. Whenever there was a housewarming or any other gathering, the young man always helped by sharing his vegetables without charge.

In addition to that, he would take his magic crystal to the new house when the gathering took place and would bless the owner with the crystal. Saying, "Today is a good day, a blessed day. We all gather here together happily. I bring this crystal with me to bless you with good fortune. I wish you luck, prosperity, and happiness ever after."

His wish was always granted. All his neighbors and friends became rich, famous, and happy. Nobody realized that all this was because of the magic of the crystal.

Now the King of China was a very powerful ruler. He wanted to widen his reign. He wanted to be the most powerful ruler in any land. One day the King asked his minister, "Dear Minister, would you please look into the future of our country and examine my horoscope. What will happen next? Will our country be peaceful and prosper?"

The Minister made his calculations, then answered, "Your Majesty, your horoscope shows that you will live a long life, but...." He stopped hesitantly. The King was curious and asked, "But what? Tell me quickly."

The Minister continued. "In the country of Thailand, there is a magic crystal. This magic crystal should be the property of the King, your Majesty. If you could get possession of this crystal, your country would prosper. You would be the most powerful ruler in any land. This crystal is in the southwest of that country, Sir."

The King laughed lightly, saying, "Is that all? That should not be difficult. Minister of Defense, send soldiers to the southwest of Thailand to find this magic crystal."

The Minister of Defense bowed and hurried out of the palace to do as the King commanded.

Soon sailing ships were sent out to search for the magic crystal. One of these ships landed in Songkla. There, they heard talk of the poor young man's good fortune. They sailed back to China to inform their King.

The King considered how he could acquire that magic crystal without starting a war with Thailand. At last, a minister suggested that the King should train a mouse to steal the magic crystal. So a tiny mouse was trained. This mouse was named "Stealy Mouse" for its great skill at theft. Stealy Mouse was very clever and very fast.

As soon as Stealy Mouse was ready, he was put aboard a ship and carried to Songkla. When the sailing ship neared the Thai shores, the captain anchored at sea and set the mouse overboard to swim to shore. Stealy Mouse went straight to the young man's hut. As it did not occur to the young man that anyone would want to steal his magic crystal, he left it lying on a shelf in plain sight.

So, there was the magic crystal, unguarded on the shelf. The young man's two dogs, Tangkuan and Noi, were running about outside playing, and the cat was chasing butterflies in the field as usual. It was an ideal time for Stealy Mouse to sneak into the hut and steal the magic crystal. Stealy Mouse hurried back to the ship, and the captain sailed straight home to China and took the magic crystal to the King. Now, because of the crystal, China became prosperous.

As for the young man, he went about his work as usual. But when he went to tend his vegetable garden, to his surprise, the vegetables were wilted and dying. He was shocked. He ran back home and found his magic crystal was gone!

The young man was very sad. He called his dogs and his cat and told them what had happened. His pets felt very sorry because they had not watched the house for him while he was gone to the fields.

Every day the poor young man thought about the handsome stranger who had given him the magic crystal. He wanted to tell the stranger about his loss. One day Khrut flew over the vegetable garden. Seeing that the vegetables were wilted and dying, he was surprised. He disguised himself as a handsome stranger once more and came to the young man's hut to ask what had happened.

The poor man was glad to see the handsome stranger again. He told what had happened, saying. "Oh, my Brother. The crystal that you gave me was stolen. I saw only the footprints of the burglar. It looked like the footprints of a mouse!"

The handsome stranger stood still for a minute. He looked at the footprints. Then he said, "Don't worry, Dear Brother. Go back home. I will bring that crystal back to you."

Khrut turned back into his true form and flew to China. There he put a spell over the entire country of China and called the magic crystal back to him. Then Khrut flew back to Thailand, turned himself into the handsome young man, and returned the crystal to the poor man once more, saying: "Please guard this carefully, Dear Brother. I must leave you."

Now that the crystal was back, the vegetables grew well again. The young man guarded his crystal carefully this time. His dogs and cat helped him guard the crystal.

As for the King of China, when he found out that his precious crystal had been stolen, he was furious. He asked the Minister what had happened. The Minister made his calculations and then said, "Dear Lord, the magic crystal has returned to its owner in Songkla."

The King was furious. He said, "Soldiers, prepare all of our fighting ships and bring that crystal back to me. I will wage war, if necessary, to get it back."

The ministers and soldiers hurried to prepare the fleet. But the King still hoped to avoid war if possible. So he said, "Minister, take Stealy Mouse with you. If the mouse can steal the crystal back without war, that would be better. Try that before you use force."

The fleet sailed for several days on the open sea, and at last reached Thailand's shore. They anchored there and, late at night, the Minister let Stealy Mouse out to swim to shore.

Stealy Mouse crept carefully all around inside the young man's hut, trying to find the crystal. Then, he saw the *pakhama* tied around the young man's waist. He knew right away that the crystal was kept there. Using his sharp teeth, Stealy Mouse bit through the *pakhama*, grabbed the crystal between its teeth, and ran from the hut.

The two dogs, awakened by the mouse's scampering, started to bark and ran after the mouse. The cat, hearing the bark, awoke and ran after the mouse too. By this time the mouse had reached the water and was swimming away, with the crystal between his teeth. The cat swam after it, got in front of the mouse, and began to claw at it. Hurt and bleeding, the mouse tried to escape onto a small island, leaving the crystal behind. But Tangkuan and Noi, the two dogs, were already on the island, blocking Stealy Mouse's way. And the cat, swimming behind the mouse now, blocked his retreat back into the sea to the waiting ships.

All day the four animals fought in this way, with the mouse unable to escape. By the end of the day, the four animals were all tired and hurt, but they continued to fight.

Just then, Khrut flew over the area and saw the King of China's fleet. He found the four animals in their miserable situation. Then he realized that he should not have given the magic crystal back to the young man. Wherever this crystal stayed, troubles would start.

To stop all of this, Khrut turned the four animals into islands and mountains. In front of Samila Beach is tiny Mouse Island, Koh Nu. The cat was turned into Cat Island, Koh Maeo. And the dogs who blocked the way to the shore rose from the sea as Tangkuan Mountain and Noi Mountain. The magic crystal, left on the beach, became white, sandy Kaeo Beach, which to this day glitters beautifully.

Seeing the damage that magic can do, Khrut left the young man to deal with his problems in his own human ways. The story of the magic crystal and Mouse Island and Cat Island became just a tale, told to later generations.

Chapter 7

Nithan Songkhruang: Elaborate Tales

Kaeo, the Horse-Face Girl

Here is a brief retelling of one of Thailand's marvelous epic fairy tales. Certainly Kaeo is a much stronger heroine than most of the European princesses we hear about. Woe to the giant or ogre who meets up with Kaeo or her daughters!

A long, long time ago, in the town of Mithila (Mee-tee-lä), Prince Pinthong (Pin-tong), the son of King Phuwadol (Poo-wä-dawl), loved to play at kites. One day, while he was flying kites with his soldiers in the palace garden, a sudden gust of wind grabbed his kite and carried it away.

Annoyed, Prince Pinthong sent his soldiers to follow that kite and retrieve it. The soldiers were just able to keep the kite in sight as they ran after it. Then, suddenly, it plummeted to the ground and disappeared. When they finally reached the spot where the kite had fallen, they saw that someone else had already found the kite. It was Kaeo, the Horse-Face Girl. Kaeo had also seen the kite fall and had run to pick it up. Now Kaeo held the kite tightly and refused to give it up.

"If this is really the kite of Prince Pinthong, then let him come to claim it himself," said Kaeo.

When a soldier carried this message back to Prince Pinthong, he was amused. He knew that Kaeo had been given her name because of her appearance. "Well let me go then and see this Horse-Face Girl who claims my kite."

Now, as soon as Kaeo, the Horse-Face Girl, saw the Prince, she fell in love with him. Her demands for the return of the kite were high. "Dear Prince, I will be glad to return your kite. But there is one condition. I would like for you to accept me as your wife in return."

The Prince was not at all pleased with this demand. He thought Kaeo, the Horse-Face Girl, was too immodest and brash. But he pretended to agree. "Very well, Kaeo, I will accept you as my wife if you return the kite. You remain here. I will return with a procession to carry you to the palace in proper style."

Kaeo was delighted. She handed over the kite and waited patiently for the Prince to return with his procession to carry her to the palace.

Of course, once the Prince returned to his palace with his kite, he gave no more thought to Kaeo, the Horse-Face Girl. Kaeo waited and waited. At last she became ill with the strain of waiting. When Kaeo's mother discovered the reason for her daughter's malaise, she determined to help.

Kaeo's mother approached the palace and asked to see King Phuwadol and the Queen. When she had related the whole story, she implored them to hold the Prince to his promise.

The Queen agreed that, indeed, Prince Pinthong must keep his promise to Kaeo. She sent a procession to bring Kaeo to the palace in style, as the Prince had promised.

But when Kaeo arrived and the King saw how very ugly she was, he could not bear to wed his son to this girl. Instead he said to Kaeo, "There are a few things I want you to do before the wedding, to prove your right to wed our royal Prince. I want you to go to Sumeru Mountain and bring me some soil from that mountain."

So Kaeo, the Horse-Face Girl, set off on the long trek to Sumeru Mountain. This was a journey of many days, but Kaeo was not daunted. She intended to wed Prince Pinthong, and she would accomplish any task set her in order to do this. One day, as she traveled on her way she passed the hut of a hermit. Kaeo devoutly stopped to pay homage to this holy man. The hermit spoke to her. "Where are you going, young woman. And why do you travel alone?"

When Kaeo had told her story, the hermit was touched by her determination. "This young woman deserves my help," he thought. To Kaeo he said, "Young woman, you must remain here with me. There are many lessons you need to learn. There is plenty of time to complete your task and wed your young man in the future. For now, remain and learn."

Kaeo was honored to be trained by this wise man. She remained with him for many months, listening and learning. The hermit taught Kaeo many things. She learned the art of curing with medicinal herbs. She learned to speak with the animals. And she learned kindness towards all living things. But lest wickedness go untamed, she also learned swordplay and the many arts of weaponry. Kaeo learned also many magic spells to use in time of need. And from the hermit she learned the art of meditation.

One last thing Kaeo learned from the hermit. She learned the art of turning herself into a young woman of great beauty. When Kaeo's learning was complete, the hermit gave her two gifts. "These will help you on your way, now that you must travel on alone." The hermit gave her a magical knife, and a marvelous flying boat.

"Thank you, Kind Hermit, for all you have taught me. And thank you for these useful gifts. Now I will get on with my quest!"

Kaeo leapt into her magical boat and flew straight to Sumeru Mountain. Kaeo took some soil from the mountain, got back into her boat, and flew back to the palace.

The King was not happy to see her return. He had assumed she was lost in the mountains, and had been glad of an excuse to wed Prince Pinthong to a lovelier wife.

"It is true that you have returned with the soil from Sumeru Mountain, as I asked. But I am afraid you are too late to marry

Prince Pinthong. At this moment he is on his way to Romewithi (Rome-wi-tee) City to marry the Princess of Romewithi."

Kaeo was not daunted. She entered a state of meditation and transformed herself into a beautiful girl. Taking the name, Mani-ratana (Mä-nee-rä-tä-nä), she climbed back into her magical boat and flew to Romewithi. The prince, traveling by land, of course, had not yet arrived. In her lovely form as Maniratana, Kaeo asked an old couple who lived by the city walls to take her in while she waited for the arrival of Prince Pinthong. This old couple was pleased with the gracious and lovely young girl and treated her as their own daughter.

When the Prince arrived in Romewithi City some time later, he was greeted by this most lovely of creatures. As soon as his eyes fell on Maniratana, he was hopelessly in love. All thoughts of the Princess of Romewithi vanished from his mind. So the Prince was wedded to Maniratana. Thus Kaeo, the Horse-Face Girl, became his bride after all.

In time, a son was born to Kaeo and Prince Pinthong. They decided to call their firstborn Pinkaeo. Soon after Pinkaeo's birth, Prince Pinthong decided to return to Mithila City to visit his parents, but disaster befell him on the way. The gruesome giants of Phalarat (Pä-lä-rät) City kidnapped Prince Pinthong as he passed through their country.

When Kaeo heard news of this horrible event, she disguised herself as a young man and took the name of Watchara (Wä-chä-rä). Kaeo climbed into her magic boat and flew straight to Phalarat City. With her magic knife, Kaeo leapt in the midst of the giants and began to slice first one and then the other. Those giants were no match for Kaeo and her magic knife. She soon had routed them. Then, still disguised as Watchara, she killed the King of the Giants himself, and freed her dear Prince Pinthong.

When Prakaimat (Prä-kai-mät), one of the king's ministers heard of the king's death, he determined to take over the realm. Now the Queen of the Giants had been widowed by Kaeo, but the thought of letting Prakaimat take over her kingdom terrified her. She appealed to Watchara to defend the kingdom against this

Prakaimat. The Queen, of course, had no idea that Watchara was really a girl in man's disguise.

Watchara and Prince Pinthong fought the wicked minister together. Those two easily defended the kingdom and restored it to the Giant Queen of Phalarat. In gratitude the Queen decided to present Watchara and Prince Pinthong with her two daughters' hands in marriage. Watchara politely declined, but Prince Pinthong graciously accepted the hands of both daughters. And so the four returned to Mithila City. Prince Pinthong, Kaeo (who now resumed her form as the lovely Maniratana), and Princess Soisuwan (Soy-su-wän) and Princess Chansuda (Jan-su-daa).

But all was not well yet. The brother of the giant minister Prakaimat gathered his troops and prepared to attack the City of Mithila. This brother, named Prakaikrot (Prä-kì-krot), wanted revenge for ... When news came of the arrival of th... and Prince Pinthong prepared to do battle ... again and nearing her time ... to fight against Prakaikro...

When ... gasped in awe. She was ind... her swords with blindin... ikrot. That creature did no... ing warrior woman. She qu... troops to flight. Then, while ... elously strong woman gave ...

ran... emchan (Jam-jan), Hi... Prä-pät-son). The girls gre... their mother, Kaeo. But on... laying in the palace gar-de... in (Pa-ya Hät-sä-deen), s... dren up in his talons, and c...

Luckily, ... r that eagle's nest. He freed the three princesses from ... cared for them. Because the three princesses were too young to travel back to Mithila City by

#310   10-18-2012 2:53PM
Item(s) checked out to p1678000.

TITLE: The rough-face girl
BARCODE: 35270000094936
DUE DATE: 11-08-12

TITLE: Young Guinevere
BARCODE: 35270000882900
DUE DATE: 11-08-12

TITLE: Sootface : an Ojibwa Cinderella s
BARCODE: 35270000882645
DUE DATE: 11-08-12

TITLE: Thai tales : folktales of Thailan
BARCODE: 35270001147295
DUE DATE: 11-08-12

RENEW : 614-251-4752 or online at
library.ohiodominican.edu/patroninfo

Kaeo, the Horse-Face Girl

themselves, the hermit raised them as best he could. As he raised the girls he taught them many skills. Magic, book learning, weaponry, medical science, all these were taught the girls as they grew. When the three girls grew into young womanhood they were as capable as any well-educated young man.

At last the day came when the three princesses were fully grown. It was time to find husbands for the three. The hermit announced throughout the land that a tournament would be held to win the hands of his three adopted daughters. In Romchak (Rome-a-jak) City lived three young princes, capable young men well known for their military prowess. They had studied with no less than Nakha, King of the Underworld. These three princes happened to pass by the hermit's hut on the very day of the tournament. The hermit had determined that the princesses themselves would fight their prospective suitors. That suitor who could outfight a princess, could wed her. These three princes and the three princesses seemed equally matched. So a tournament was held.

They fought first with *krabong* (krä-bong), long rods. It was soon clear that neither the princes nor the princesses would defeat the other at this match. So they moved to closer fighting with the short rods. Here too they were evenly matched.

Now the fighting became more serious as the princesses drew their long swords, *krabi* (krä-bee). Once again the six were evenly matched. So, finally, the princesses drew short swords and moved in on their opponents again. But still, neither princes nor princesses could gain an advantage. Each tried all the tricks they knew. All of the things taught them by their teachers came into play in this battle. But throughout it all, they remained equally matched. Neither side could win.

At last the hermit called a halt to the fighting. The match was perfect. The three princesses were given in marriage to the three princes.

Meanwhile, Prince Pinkaeo had attained his manhood. As the eldest son of Kaeo, the Horse-Face Girl, and Prince Pinthong, he set out to find his three younger sisters, who had not been seen since the wicked eagle kidnapped them so many years ago. Tracking that eagle, he at last reached its nest. There he learned of the hermit who had raised the three young girls.

At last, he discovered his sisters, the three princesses, and all were reunited. He was pleased with their happy marriages to the three princes. All returned to Mithila City to be reunited with their father Prince Pinthong and their mother, Kaeo, the Horse-Face Girl. Thus the entire family Pinthong lived happily ever after.

Chet Huat Chet Hai
(Seven Pot, Seven Jar)

Even though Chet Huat Chet Hai's parents treat him poorly in the story's beginning, he cares for them properly at the tale's end. It is important in Thai culture to take good care of your parents. Regardless of how parents act, it is the duty of the children to look after them.

The *chingrit* which our heroes catch and eat are insects resembling crickets, though they are larger and much tastier than crickets.

A long, long time ago a poor couple lived near the edge of the forest. They were so poor they barely had enough rice to eat. And to make matters worse, their only son was an unusual boy with exceptional strength. He needed lots of food. Ever since he had reached the age of seven, he had eaten an enormous amount of food each day. For only one meal he consumed seven pots of rice and seven jars of salted fish! So he was called "Chet Huat Chet Hai," or "Seven Pot, Seven Jar."

The poor couple tried hard to provide for their son, but they could not seem to get ahead. Every day, that son needed his seven pots of rice and seven jars of salted fish to fill his stomach. Finally, the poor couple decided they could no longer provide for their son. They quietly consulted each other.

"Let us leave him in the forest," the father said.

"Oh, but he will be frightened and hungry at night, " the mother protested.

"Then what do you suggest?" the father asked.

"I do not want him to suffer. He is still too young to fend for himself," the mother said.

Several nights later, the couple found themselves faced with the son's eating habit again. There was no food left in the house. They did not know where the next meal would come from. There was just no way they could feed a child with such a huge appetite. Then the father said, "Tomorrow, I will take him into the forest with me. If it is necessary, I will kill him myself to spare him from hunger." The mother sobbed quietly, but did not say anything. The next morning the father asked his son to go into the forest with him.

"Chet Huat Chet Hai, you are a big boy now. You can help your father fell a tree for firewood to sell at the market. So be ready in five minutes."

Chet Huat Chet Hai was glad to be of help to his old father. He hurriedly dressed and waited excitedly for his father. Once they reached the deep forest, the father found a tall tree and started to cut it. When the tree was about to fall, the father told his son, "Chet Huat Chet Hai, when the tree falls, you try to catch it. We do not want any marks on the tree. This tree is too beautiful to use as firewood. We can sell it as lumber to build houses with. Remember, catch the tree. Do not let it fall to the ground."

Chet Huat Chet Hai obediently did as he was told. Unfortunately, the tree was so big that when it fell on top of Chet Huat Chet Hai, its weight pushed Chet Huat Chet Hai down under the earth. The impact was earthshattering. The sound of the falling tree was earsplitting.

Even though the father had planned this accident, now that it had happened, he began to cry uncontrollably. He ran over to where his son had disappeared but he could not see Chet Huat Chet Hai because the huge tree was on top of him. The father thought his son was surely crushed to death. He prayed quietly for his son and began the journey home to tell his wife.

Even before he reached home, he saw his son come running after him, carrying the great tree. "I'm coming, Father! Where do you want the tree carried?" When the tree had fallen on Chet Huat Chet Hai he had been stunned by the blow for a few moments. But as soon as he had recovered, he had hurried to push the huge

Chet Huat Chet Hai (Seven Pot, Seven Jar)

tree off of his body, strip off its branches, and lift it up to carry it home. The father was both glad and dismayed to see his son still alive. But he did not say anything. He went inside and asked his wife to find something for his son to eat.

The next day, the father asked his son to go into the forest with him again. This time he said he wanted his son to help him catch a horse.

"Son, if we can catch a wild horse, we can sell it in the market, or we could use it on our farm."

Once they had reached the deep forest, the father led his son to a wide river. "Son, this is the river where wild animals come to drink. Stay here and wait to catch a wild horse. I will go look upriver." The father hurried home in tears, believing that wild animals would soon come and kill his son.

Chet Huat Chet Hai did not know what a horse looked like. He obediently waited by the river for a long time. When he saw a tiger coming down to drink, he thought this must be a horse. He caught the tiger bare-handed, tied the tiger's legs, and sat waiting for his father's return. When the sun set and the father did not return, he began to worry. He thought, "I should go home and tell my mother." So he untied the tiger, jumped on its back, and rode the tiger home.

When he arrived home, the tiger was roaring loudly. The dog and the chickens were terrified and fled into the forest. They never returned. That is why some of these domesticated animals are wild.

The couple was very frightened when they saw their son on the back of the tiger. They called out, "Son, get away from the tiger. Let it go free in the forest. Do not bring it home!"

Chet Huat Chet Hai did not understand all this, but he obediently did as he was told.

Many months later, the couple consulted each other, "We are so poor. There is no more rice, no more fish. We cannot provide enough food for ourselves and our eat-too-much son. How can we go on living?" They decided the only solution was to try to abandon their son again.

The next morning, the mother called her son. "Son, we have run out of money to buy food. There is nothing left to eat. I need money to buy food and the giant owes me money. Can you go ask him to pay me now?" She thought Chet Huat Chet Hai would never return from such a trip. The son felt sorry for his poor parents. "Do not worry, Mother. I will go to the giant and bring back the money."

So it was that Chet Huat Chet Hai began his great adventure. He set off in search of the giant. Chet Huat Chet Hai hadn't gone far when he heard a loud rumbling sound from the road ahead. Climbing the hill, he looked down and saw a remarkable sight. A man was coming up the road pulling a cartload of bricks. But fastened behind that cart was *another* cartload of bricks, and behind *that* cart was *another*. This man was pulling 100 cartloads of bricks up the hill, all by himself!

"Good day," said Chet Huat Chet Hai. "My name is Chet Huat Chet Hai, and I am searching for the giant. But who on earth are *you*?"

"My name is Kwian Roi Lem, 'One Hundred Carts.' I am so strong that I can pull 100 carts at a time with ease. I also like to fight giants. Could I go with you?"

"Certainly!" Chet Huat Chet Hai was glad to have a companion. So the two set out in search of the giant.

Soon they heard a strange cracking and crashing sound ahead. There on the river bank was a man felling bamboos. But instead of cutting them, he was pulling them up like weeds. He was grabbing 100 bamboos at a time, yanking them from the soil, and tossing them aside!

"Good day, I am Chet Huat Chet Hai, and this is my companion Kwian Roi Lem, we are traveling to fight the giant. But who are you?"

"They call me Phai Roi Ko, 'One Hundred Bamboos' because I can pull 100 bamboos at a time. I would like to fight the giant too. Could I go with you?"

"Certainly, we would like another companion."

Chet Huat Chet Hai (**Seven Pot, Seven Jar**)

So the three companions traveled on together. After a while they heard a loud chopping noise coming from the forest ahead. "A woodsman is at work," said Chet Huat Chet Hai. But when they approached the woodsman, they saw a remarkable sight. This man had no axe. He was whacking the trees with his head to fell them!

"Good day, I am Chet Huat Chet Hai and these are my companions Kwian Roi Lem and Phai Roi Ko. We are traveling to conquer the giant. But who are you?"

"Huo Tok Ki, 'Head Stronger than an Axe' is my name. As you see, my head is so strong that I don't need an axe to cut down trees. I like to fight giants too. May I go with you?" The companions were delighted with their new friend and the four set off on their way.

Clearly, these four young men were well suited for each other. They vowed to support each other come what may. If one was ever in trouble, the others would help him out. But there was no food in the land through which they were traveling.

After they had traveled for two days without food, they were so hungry they decided to dig some *chingrit* bugs to eat. Today, chingrit resemble large crickets. But at that time this was not a small insect as it is now. The chingrit of those days were as big as elephants! Chet Huat Chet Hai let his three friends try first to catch the chingrit. The huge insects were very strong. They kicked loose each time one of the strong men tried to hold them. But when Chet Huat Chet Hai tried, he succeeded in digging an insect from its hole and dragging it out.

However, they could not eat the chingrit raw, and they had no fire to roast their food. A house roof could be seen in the distance, so Chet Huat Chet Hai sent one of his strong companions to fetch fire from its inhabitant.

Unfortunately, that house happened to be the home of an evil sorceress. She possessed many powers, including a magic life-and-death stick. If she pointed the death end at a person, that person fell dead. If she pointed the life end at a dead person, that person came back to life. This sorceress sat all day crouched like a spider over a huge weaving of sticky silken strands. All day she wove these strands in and out, and if a stranger ventured near, she hurled the long silken strands over him, drew him near, and bound him tight in her weaving.

When the unsuspecting Kwian Roi Lem approached, the sorceress invited him in sweetly. "But come a little closer, I will be glad to lend you some fire." Thus she enticed him nearer and nearer to the spot where she sat weaving, then, suddenly, she lashed out with her strands and enveloped him in a mesh of silk, trapping the strong young man.

Chet Huat Chet Hai waited a long time for his friend to return with the fire, then he sent a second companion. Phai Roi Ko met the same fate. And Huo Tok Ki followed soon after. Seeing that none of his companions returned, Chet Huat Chet Hai suspected foul play. He hurried to see what had happened.

He approached the house of the sorceress carefully, looking to see what might have happened to his friends. "Have you seen my three friends?" he called to the weaving sorceress. "I sent them to borrow fire from you so we could cook our meat. They did not return."

The sorceress beckoned to Chet Huat Chet Hai. "Come closer young man. Your friends are right here. See, I am keeping them tight in my silken strands. Come closer and you will see." She meant to capture Chet Huat Chet Hai in her silken strands also, but she was mistaken. He watched her movements carefully, and when she threw her silk threads he was ready. Chet Huat Chet Hai jumped aside nimbly. Then, before she could recoil her strands to throw again, he pounced on the sorceress and quickly wrestled her into submission. Wrapping her in her own sticky silk, he bound her tight.

Then Chet Huat Chet Hai picked up the magic life-and-death stick. "Which end is which?" He pointed the death end toward the witch. That was the end of her. Then he reversed the stick and pointed the life end toward each of his companions. Chet Huat Chet Hai pulled his revived friends from the silken mess and the four gathered embers from the fire of the sorceress and hurried back to cook their dinner.

Made strong once more by the tasty chingrit dinner, the four friends set off to find the giant. After traveling for some time, they reached a town where everyone was huddling in fright. "Why is everyone here so frightened?" asked the friends.

"A giant has been coming every day to eat one of us. He catches one person each day for his meal. He is so powerful we cannot conquer him."

At last they had found the giant. "Do not worry," said the four companions. "We have come to fight your giant. When he comes tomorrow he will eat no one. We guarantee it."

"Our king has sent many brave men to fight the giant," said the townsfolk. "No one has succeeded. He has promised that anyone who defeats the giant will marry the princess and have the throne of the kingdom."

"Well that is fine with us!" laughed the four companions.

The next day, when the giant came stomping down the hill, drooling for his meal, the four companions were ready. Chet Huat Chet Hai leaped onto the giant and held him fast. Using his head as an axe, Huo Tok Ki, quickly chopped the giant in two in the middle. Phai Roi Ko pulled off the giant's limbs as if they had been 100 bamboos. And Kwian Roi Lem hauled away the giant's body easily, though it weighed as much as 100 cartloads of bricks.

The king and his subjects were ecstatic. "Come and claim your prize!" they called.

The four friends consulted. It was decided that Chet Huat Chet Hai, as leader of the group, would marry the princess. The other three friends were each given an important post in the kingdom, and for many years, the town prospered under the rule of these four strong friends.

But Chet Huat Chet Hai was thinking of his poor parents. He sent for them and told them, "Dear Father and Mother, you don't have to worry about me any more. I am capable of taking care of myself now. I am ruler of my own kingdom and I can afford to eat as much as I want. You have taken care of me for many years. Now it is my turn to take care of you."

From then on Chet Huat Chet Hai made sure that his parents lived in comfort and had plenty of food to eat.

This is the happy ending of the tale of Chet Huat Chet Hai, the boy who ate seven pots of rice and seven jars of salted fish at one sitting.

Chapter 8

Thep Niyai: Tales of Helpful Gods and Spirits

The Twin Stars

The story of the cowherd and the spinning maid is known in many Asian countries. In Japan and in parts of China and Korea this story is an important part of folk festival celebrations on the Seventh Day of the Seventh Moon. In Thailand, the story is told, but no special celebration occurs.

The *Phra In* (Prä In) of this tale is the Indian god Indra.

Once upon a time, the King of Heaven, Phra In, had a beautiful niece. She was a most lovely heavenly being and also a very diligent worker. She was known for her spinning and weaving abilities. All of the fine fabric which this goddess created, she gave away to others.

One day, Phra In spoke to his niece, "Dear Niece, you are now a fully grown woman. It is time you thought of marrying. Is there some heavenly being with whom you are in love? If so, just let me know and I will arrange the wedding."

The niece stopped and pondered Phra In's words. "Give me time, Dear Uncle. Let me consider whom I want to have as a husband. Then I will give you my answer."

From that time on, the niece traveled about, looking for the perfect mate. She traveled all of the heavens, but she did not find one heavenly being to whom she wished to be married. Then, one day, as she was flying over the earth, she heard the sound of a lonely flute rising from a pasture. The sound of this flute was so entrancing that she was drawn near to the flute player. Who should it be but a lowly cowherd, sitting by his cows and playing his flute. At this time, Fate took a hand. The heavenly maid fell instantly in love with the lowly human cowherd. She sat entranced, listening to his music. She had no longing to return to her heavenly home, but wished only to stay by the side of this young man.

Phra In (Pra-In)—the King of Heaven who sits on a very soft throne. If there is trouble in the world, Phra In's throne becomes suddenly as hard as a rock. Phra In is alerted and looks down on earth to see what problems need solving.

When his niece told Phra In of her decision, he agreed to allow the wedding. Even the gods sometimes smile on the course of true love.

Once the lovers were married, the heavenly maid spent her days on earth. She, herself, lived as a human being. And as the wife of a lowly cowherd, her duties were many. Each day, she must care for the house, the farm, the cows, and her new husband. There was little time left for her own spinning and weaving. She was no longer able to produce the yards of lovely fabric which had been such fine gifts.

Whenever Phra In glanced down to earth, he saw his dear niece at work cleaning the house, or weeding their small fields. And when she was not working, she spent her time laughing and talking with her new husband. Her loom stood unused in a corner of their hut. No more did beautiful fabric flow from her skilled fingers. Clearly, Phra In had to do something about this state of affairs.

Taking a piece of paper in hand, Phra In inscribed an edict ordering the young lovers to see each other only once every seven days. "If they meet but once a week, that should give her some time to continue her spinning and weaving," he thought.

The crow was summoned to carry this edict down to earth and deliver it to the young lovers. But as the way to earth was long, the crow stopped en route to rest. He laid down the letter, and took his ease for a while. Suddenly, a vulture swooped by overhead. The crow, in a panic at the sight of this huge bird of prey, flew off. But in his fright, he left the letter behind. By the time he remembered his mission, the letter was lost, and no amount of searching could turn it up.

The crow dared not return to Phra In and report his failing. But he thought of a way out of his trouble. Fetching paper and pen, the crow simply rewrote the letter. "Edict: From this day on, the young lovers are to meet only once every seven...." Here the crow's memory became a little foggy. "Oh yes, every seven months. No.... There had been something about days in there too ... on the seventh day of the seventh month." And this is the message which the crow delivered to our young lovers. Of course, they were heartbroken at such an edict. But the word of Phra In cannot be ignored. The lovers separated. And from that time on, they met only once every year.

Phra In was surprised to see this development. He called the couple to him and questioned them. It was then that he discovered the failing of the crow. In his great anger he summoned the crow and pronounced a terrible sentence. From that time on the crow must live only on earth. Never more could he fly in the heavenly realms. And once every year, on the seventh day of the seventh month, the poor crow would lose all of its feathers! At that time it must sit miserably in its nest, and not fly about at all. Such a molting was the faithless bird's fate.

As for the lovers, Phra In could not rescind the edict. A law of Phra In, once issued, could not be broken, even by its maker himself. So Phra In turned the ill-fated lovers into stars and set them both in the sky. There they remain to this day, shining far apart. But every year, according to the edict of Phra In, as rewritten by the crow, the lovers meet for one brief night ... on the seventh day of the seventh moon.

Songkran: A Thai New Year Story

Songkran (Songkrän) is the Thai New Year celebration. It takes place on April 13-15 each year. This story is remembered each year at Songkran time.

When Buddhism spread throughout Thailand, the Buddhist religion did not attempt to stamp out the Hindu beliefs already there. Nor did they attempt to suppress animistic beliefs in nature spirits, which predated even the Hindu religion. In this New Year myth we see Buddhist concepts such as the "cool heart" or calm nature, Hindu gods, and a tree spirit, all in one story.

The *Sai* (Si) tree in this story is a type of fig tree. It was believed that a *rukkha-thewada (rookä-tewädä),* a tree deity, or nature spirit, dwelled in any large or impressive looking tree.

In the Hindu heaven there are 16 heavens, each ruled by a different *prom* (prom). Thao Kabinlaphrom (Käbinläprom), or Brahma, rules the highest heaven. He is known for always keeping his word and he meditates constantly. Because of these qualities, he creates supernatural energy which causes his head to become very hot.

Phra In (Prä In) is the Hindu god Indra, the King of Heaven. He sits on a very soft throne. If there is trouble in the world, Phra In's throne becomes suddenly as hard as a rock. Phra In is alerted and looks down on earth to see what problem needs solving.

Thammaban (Täm-mä-bän) in our story is a holy creature lower than the gods, yet above the humans. He could be compared to the Buddhist Boddhisattva, an individual who has attained enlightenment and is able to help others. Thammaban is known for descending to earth to help those in need.

This story includes a riddle about *rasi (rä-see).* This concept can be described as a person's inner glow. Beauty, glory, wellbeing, grace, all of these terms are used to speak of *rasi.* If a person has *rasi,* it is apparent to all who see that individual.

It was told and retold a long time ago, this story of a rich man and a poor drunkard who were neighbors. The rich man had no children, but the drunkard had two beautiful, healthy children.

One day the drunkard insulted the rich man. The rich man was perplexed by the drunkard's rude behavior. He was not angry, but rather annoyed. He asked, "Dear Neighbor, why do you insult me? Why are you rude to me, your neighbor? I am wealthy and should be respected, not insulted."

The drunkard scornfully answered, "You think you are rich because you have lots of money. But you are also poor, because you have no children. When you die, your money will be of no use to you. I may seem poor, because I have no money. But I have two sons. They will carry on my name. When I pass away from this world, my name will still be mentioned. I feel much richer than you."

The rich man listened carefully, thoughtfully. He was, after all, a level-headed and reasonable man with a "cool heart." After giving the drunkard's words some thought, he had to agree with him. Yes, he himself was a poor man, because he had no sons to inherit his wealth and carry on his name. He felt sorry for himself and his wife then. He decided he too must have a son.

Phra Prom (Phra-Prom)—one of the gods who rules the highest heaven.

Thep Niyai: **Tales of Helpful Gods and Spirits**

From that day on, the rich man tried to have a son. He prayed to the gods, the deities, the sun, and the moon. He faithfully worshipped all heavenly bodies. Three years passed. Still his wife did not conceive.

One Songkran Day, when the sun was shining brightly in the sky, the rich man, accompanied by his many servants, went to a large sai tree near the river bank. This huge *Sai* tree was occupied by many birds. The rich man ordered his servants to clean the rice seven times, then cook the rice. Once the rice was cooked, he offered it to the *Sai* tree. He had arranged for lively music to celebrate the occasion. Once again, he made his wish. "Please, God of the Sai Tree, grant me a son."

Now the forest deity who resided in this sai tree heard the man's wish. He saw that the rich man was a good man who sincerely wanted to have a son. The deity took pity on the rich man, therefore, he flew up to Phra In in heaven and said, "Please, Phra In, please grant this rich man a son. Please send some god or angel down to be this rich man's son."

Phra In looked down to earth and saw the rich man's sincerity. He agreed that the rich man should indeed have a son. So he ordered Thammaban to go down and become the rich man's son. Not long after this, the wife of the rich man conceived and gave birth to a healthy and beautiful son. The rich man named this son Thammaban Kuman which meant "Thammaban son."

The rich man ordered an architect to build a large palace for his only son. The house was seven stories tall. It was built near the *Sai* tree by the river bank. Thammaban Kuman grew up in this seven-storied palace. He listened often to the singing of the birds who lived in the branches of the *Sai* tree, and after a while, he began to understand their language. Thammaban was quick in all of his learning, science, and literature. By the time he was seven years old, he had completed his formal education. Thammaban became a teacher himself at that early age. People came to listen to his teachings and to hear Thammaban's predictions for the future. His advice was always wise. News of the wisdom and kindness of this child prodigy spread over the land.

At that time, most villagers worshipped Thao Kabinlaphrom. They went to this god for guidance and instruction. But more and more people started going to Thammaban Kuman for his wise teachings. This displeased the god.

Thao Kabinlaphrom decided to come down from heaven and test Thammaban Kuman. He proposed a contest. "If you can answer my three questions, I, Thao Kabinlaphrom, will cut off my own head. If you cannot solve these problems, then I will behead you."

He posed his questions.

"In the morning, where is a man's *rasi*?"

"At noon, where is a man's *rasi*?"

"In the evening, where is a man's *rasi*?"

Thammaban Kuman could not answer right away. This *rasi* referred to man's inner beauty, his sense of grace. Thammaban Kuman carefully said, "Please give me time to think about these three questions. I will give you the answer in seven days." Six days passed. Thammaban Kuman still could not solve the problems. He began to despair. He thought, "Tomorrow, I surely will be beheaded. If I do not want to be killed by Kabinlaphrom, I should try to escape. But should I do this?"

Undecided, he went out of his palace. He walked to the *Sai* tree and sat down under its huge branches. Now in the *Sai* tree lived a pair of eagles. When night fell, the wife asked her husband, "Dear Husband, tomorrow where will we go to find our food?"

"No problem, my dear," answered her husband. "Tomorrow we can wait right here. Tomorrow we can consume Thammaban Kuman for our food. He is sure to be beheaded by Kabinlaphrom. He will never solve the questions."

"What are the questions, dear?"

"The questions are three: 'In the morning, where is a man's *rasi*? At noon, where is a man's *rasi*? In the evening, where is a man's *rasi*?'"

The female eagle thought about that for a while, then she asked: "Dear Husband, what is the answer to these questions? I cannot solve them."

Patiently, the husband explained. "It is like this, my dear. In the morning, a man's *rasi* is on his face. That is why men wash their faces in the morning when they rise. At noon, a man's *rasi* is on his chest. That is why men sprinkle fragrant water on their chests. In the evening, a man's *rasi* is on his feet. That is why men wash their feet before going to bed."

Thammaban Kuman, lying under the *Sai* tree, heard every word that the two eagles spoke. He hurried excitedly back to his palace and waited for the visit of Thao Kabinlaphrom the next day. When Thao Kabinlaphrom heard these answers, he was amazed. They were absolutely correct. Thao Kabinlaphrom always kept his word. He would follow his own agreement. He would behead himself. But before he took his own head, he asked to see his seven daughters. These daughters served as Phra In's handmaidens.

"Dear Daughters, I will take my own head as I promised to Thammaban Kuman. But my head, as you know, is the center of all heat in the universe. If my head falls to the ground, fire will spread over the world. If my head is thrown into the air, the weather will become so dry that no rain will ever fall again. If my head drops into the ocean, the seas will all dry up. Therefore, my dear seven daughters, I ask that you take turns carrying a tray on which my head will rest. Each of you may carry this tray in turn, for 365 days."

After making these arrangements, Thao Kabinlaphrom fulfilled his pledge, and beheaded himself. His eldest daughter caught his fallen head, placed it on her tray, and carried it off. For 60 days she flew, circling Mount Sumeru, holding the tray in her hands. Then she set the tray in a cave on Mount Kraita. There she paid homage to her father's severed head, putting flowers and incense sticks around it. Vetsukam (Vet-sook-am), God of the Builders, came to build a crystal building around the head. He used seven kinds of crystal in this construction, and he called the building "Phakkawadi" (Pä-kä-wä-dee). This building was then used as a meeting place for the gods and angels. Every 365 days, another of Thao Kabinlaphrom's daughters takes over guardianship of her father's head. When the head passes on to another daughter, a full Thai year is said to have passed.

The Daughters of Thao Kabinlaphrom and Their Attributes

The seven daughters of Thao Kabinlaphrom are honored on Songkran Day. If Songkran falls on a Sunday, Thungsa (Toong-sä) is honored. Her special flower is the *thapthim*, which she wears on her ear. Her jewel is the red ruby, and her food is the fig. In her right hand, she holds a *chak* (chak), a serrated disc for throwing as a weapon; in her left, a *sang* weapon, a conch shell. She rides *Khrut* (Garuda), the half-man, half-bird mythical creature.

If Songkran falls on a Monday, Khorak (Ko-räk) is honored. She wears a *peap* flower on her ear, and a *mukda*, a cloudy black jewel, as her ornament. Oil is her food. Her weapons are a short sword for the right hand and a cane stick for the left. She rides on the tiger.

If Songkran falls on a Tuesday, Raksot (Räk-sat) is honored. A lotus is her flower; her ornament is the precious stone *mora*. Blood is her food. Weapons for Raksot are a *trisoon*, a trident on her right hand, and a bow on her left. She rides a hog.

If Songkran falls on a Wednesday, Mantha (Manthä) is honored. She wears the *champa* flower on her ear. Her ornament is the precious stone *phaitoon*. Her foods are cheese and butter. Her weapons are a needle for her right hand and a cane stick for her left. She rides on a donkey.

When Songkran falls on a Thursday, Kirini (Kee-ree-nee) is honored. A *montha* flower is worn on her ear. Her ornament is an emerald. Her foods are beans and sesame seeds. Her weapons are a hook for her right hand and a lyre for her left. She rides an elephant.

When Songkran falls on a Friday, Kimitha (Kee-mee-tä) is honored. Her flower is the *chongkonlani*, her ornament the yellow topaz. Her food is banana. Her weapons are a *chak* for her right hand and a lyre for her left. She rides the water buffalo.

When Songkran falls on a Saturday, Mahothon (Ma-ho-ton) is honored. She wears a *samhaw* flower on her ear. Her ornament is the black sapphire. Her food is venison. In her right hand she holds a *chak*, and in her left a *trisoon* as her weapons. She rides the peacock.

Through the hands of these seven maidens, the fiery head of Thao Kabinlaphrom is guarded and passed on from year to year.

Chapter 9

The Place of Buddhism in Thai Life

Buddhist Concepts

Buddhism is the national religion of Thailand. About 95% of Thai are Buddhist, therefore Buddhist religion plays an important part in Thai lives. The Thai constitution provides that the king must be Buddhist, and important ritual days of the Buddhist calendar have been declared national holidays.

Many of the tales in this collection illustrate Buddhist thought. Here is a discussion of some important Buddhist concepts which you may see at work in our stories.

Tham Boon, Making Merit

The Thai Buddhists believe that one should make or accumulate merit to improve oneself. *Tham boon,* or merit making, helps one to be happy and content with one's life. The amount of merit one gains in this life will be rewarded in the next life. One gains merit by such acts as entering the monkhood or novicehood for a period of time, by offering food to the monks, by caring for and protecting the sick and the poor, by being generous, gentle, sympathetic, compassionate, considerate, serene, impartial, modest, kind, and friendly. These acts gain merit for one and speed one's progress toward *Nirvana,* the Enlightenment.

Plongtok, Acceptance

The Thai Buddhist tends to accept life as it comes. It is believed that one's own *karma,* the nature of past deeds, brings about one's fate. *Karma,* to the Buddhist, is a universal law of cause and effect. One is solely responsible for his or her own *karma.* Wrong deeds accumulate bad *karma.* Good deeds are rewarded with good. If not in this life, then in the next.

Attahi Attano Natho, Self-Reliance

Buddhism counsels the individual to be self-reliant. *"Attahi attano natho"* means "You yourself are your helper." You are free to choose how to act, and your actions directly effect your *karma*. As the old adage says *"Tham dee dai dee, Tham chua dai chua,"* "Do good, receive good. Do evil, receive evil." In other words, one reaps what one sows. One reaps joy and sorrow as a result of thoughts and deeds. This result may not be immediate, but it will be rewarded at some time in the future. Because one's fate lies in one's own hand, one can improve his or her *karma* and change the course of existence.

One should meet every situation adequately. One relies on oneself and one's ability to improve one's situation in life. "Be lamps unto yourself" said Buddha. This means one must save oneself. Nobody else can do that for you.

Chai Yen, Self-Restraint

Buddhism emphasizes the positive virtue of avoiding the extremes of the emotional spectrum. *Chai yen,* or the "cool heart," is the exercise of self-restraint and self-control. One should curb one's expressions of anti-social feelings. Theoretically, this applies to any emotions: love, hatred, friendship, anger, annoyance, or to any actions: eating, sleeping, talking, and so on. One should live in moderation in all ways, emotionally and physically. This Thai tranquility and restraint, or the *chai yen* concept, is rooted in Buddhist ideals. The Thai are willing to accept, rather than challenge, because acceptance is not only safer, but also more decent, more graceful than rebellion. The Thai try to harmonize rather than compete with their physical environment and in their interpersonal relationships.

Mai Pen Rai, "Never Mind"

Whenever something does not go the way it is supposed to, the Thai usually just say *"Mai pen rai,"* "Never mind," or "It does not matter." This shows politeness and a willingness to smooth things out and avoid conflict. It also gives a sense of aloofness or noninvolvement and acceptance. Because the Thai want to keep relationships peaceful and on an even keel, they shrug off the little frustrations and disagreements of life to prevent anger or passion from coming to the surface. The Thai Buddhist believes that all things must pass. Nothing stays the same. Tomorrow will be better if one copes the best one can today. One practices tolerance and a sympathetic mind when one says, *"Mai pen rai."*

Kreng Chai, Consideration

Based on Buddhist attitudes of benevolence and respect for others, the Thai seek to insure that in face-to-face situations, no one is placed in a position of embarrassment or shame. To be considerate, *kreng chai,* is a valued character trait of the Thai. Criticism, coercion, and pressure should be avoided in order that all relationships may be pleasant and relaxed. Equanimity and "right speech" play an important role in the *kreng chai* concept.

Respect for Elders

The Thai emphasize the importance of paying respect to one's elders, whether this respect is earned through age or status. Showing respect for one's elders is a valued character trait. It could be said that the Thai are status conscious in this respect. When one passes one's elders, one should lower one's body, or even kneel or crawl, to pass. One should not sit or stand higher than one's elders. One usually calls one's elder by an honorary title, such as Lung (uncle), Pa (aunt), Ta (grandfather), or Yai (grandmother), even though the person so addressed may not be an actual blood relative.

Humbleness and Gentleness

Being humble and gentle is another character trait valued by the Thai. One learns at a very young age not to be boastful, to downplay one's self, and to carefully control body movements. One learns to be gentle and avoid the extremes of emotion, and to be considerate of other people's feelings. One learns to control one's mind, remaining impartial and serene. Buddhist religion is a religion of peace. It teaches its practitioners to be peaceful and content.

Monkhood

In Thailand, *Sangkha,* or brotherhood of monks, is the third of the Three Treasures of Buddhism. The first is The Buddha, the second is *Dharma.* To "take on a yellow robe," or become a monk, is considered a highly meritorious act. The man's parents will surely be lifted to heaven by his act.

Any man can become a Buddhist monk after he reaches 20 years of age. Before reaching that age, he may become only a *samanera,* or novice. However, ordination either as a monk or as a novice does not necessitate an everlasting vow. A monk or a novice may leave his monastic order at any time he likes, provided he goes through the proper rites. Thai custom encourages every man to spend a part of his life in a Buddhist monastery as a monk. There he learns Buddhist scriptures and follows a strict code of monastic regulations. He learns to train himself in self-restraint and self-control against worldly temptation, and to discipline himself in the Buddhist way of life, free from all forms of hate and revenge. This discipline is regarded as a very important element of life, so much so that a man who once entered monkhood is considered a fully mature man, a learned man or *Khon Suk* (literally a "ripe man"). He is then ready to marry and live a full life. Those who never become monks are considered immature or *Khon Dip* ("unripe man").

This custom of each man entering into monkhood for a few months of his life keeps the *Sangkha* in close touch with the people. Thus the mild and gentle spirit of Buddhism is spread far and wide throughout the country and has penetrated the hearts and minds of the Thai people. This practice helps the young man encircle and control his feelings and seek a quiet, peaceful life. The yellow robed Buddhist monks are a constant reminder to the Thai people of the spiritual side of life.

Moreover, Buddhist monks are involved in all aspects of life among the Thai. They make their rounds early each morning with their bowls. This is not considered begging, but is giving people a chance to make merit by offering food. People learn to become generous when they learn to share. At the housewarming ceremony and other Thai rites, monks are usually invited to come to chant and to bless the house and the people by sprinkling sacred water. On Sabbath day at the monastery or *wat*, monks chant and tell stories of the many lives of Buddha or tell moral tales based on Buddhist scriptures. For centuries, before formal education was enforced in 1898, monasteries provided free education for boys in Thailand. The monks served as teachers. The teaching monk, *achan*, taught literature, mathematics, science, and religion and also acted as role model for his students. In fact, the Lord Buddha himself was highly revered as a Model Teacher.

The Buddhist Philosophy

Samsara, The Wheel of Life

In the Buddhist view, all things, including life, are transitory. Everything is *anitchung*, or transient. Life is full of suffering or conflict (*thukkhang*), and is without essence, in other words, life is non-self (*anatta*). Existence is only a continuous process of change. Nothing which has form can endure for eternity. Sooner or later it will change. New, old, worn, disintegrated, young, old, sick, and dying, nothing lasts forever. Everything changes from one form to another. Because of earthly cravings and ignorance, one is caught on the Wheel of Life (*Samsara*). This means one is reborn again and again. Only by overcoming these earthly cravings and our ignorance can we attain *Nirvana*, the Awakening or the Enlightenment.

One tries to overcome the Wheel of Life by doing good, avoiding evil, and purifying one's mind.

The Way of Buddha, or the Path Toward Enlightenment

One can improve his lot by understanding *Dharma*, The Way of Buddha. The essence of *Dharma* is expressed in these Four Noble Truths:

1. Existence is suffering, and suffering is unavoidable.

2. Suffering is caused by desire.

3. The elimination of desire will bring suffering to an end.

4. There is a means to eliminate desire and thus suffering. It is called The Eightfold Path or The Middle Way.

The Eightfold Path, or The Middle Way

1. *Right speech*. Open, kind, truthful talk. Do not say anything that may displease others even though it may be completely true. This quality is part of *krang chai*, consideration.

2. *Right conduct*. Peaceful, honest, pure, without killing any living things, without stealing. Living in harmony with your surroundings.

3. *Right livelihood*. An honest occupation, earning a living without bringing suffering, hurt, or danger to any living thing.

4. *Right effort*. Effort in self-restraint and self-control. Constantly appraise and discipline yourself. Overcome greed, hatred, ill will, and delusion.

5. *Right mindfulness*. Achieve a watchful mind, remember that all things are transient, accept suffering and non-self. The Buddhist ideal is to become detached from the material world and to cultivate thoughts of loving kindness, compassion, sympathy, and equanimity.

6. *Right concentration*. Deep meditation on the realities of life. Maintain a clear and peaceful mind.

7. *Right views*. Know what is good and what is evil.

8. *Right intentions*. Be free from greed, hatred, cruelty, violence. Constantly examine your own motives and feelings toward others.

Five Rules of Conduct for Laymen

To make the expected behavior absolutely clear, five basic laws are given which even the least devout are expected to live by. Monks, of course, are expected to attain a much higher level of religious behavior. The Buddhist five basic precepts for the layman are:

1. Do not kill any living things.
2. Do not steal.
3. Do not act unchastely.
4. Do not lie.
5. Do not drink intoxicating beverages.

Prom Wihan

In simplest terms, Buddhist morality involves avoiding evil, doing good, and purifying one's mind. However the Buddhist *ideal* is to become detached from the material world and to cultivate the ethical ideals of loving kindness, compassion, sympathetic joy, and equanimity. These qualities are known as *Prom wihan*, the four sublime states of consciousness.

Thailand, The Land of Smiles

Foreigners have nicknamed Thailand "The Land of Smiles" because Thai people smile a lot. The famous Thai smiles mean many things. A smile may show that one is happy, pleasant, relaxed, and friendly. A smile may show contentment with life and the world. A smile may also show that the Thai tolerate the inconveniences and the displeasures of life with good humor. A smile may indicate an effort to smooth things over and maintain a pleasant relationship. The Thai do not like confrontation, they would rather suppress personal dissatisfaction and annoyance and cover it with a smile.

The Thai love *sanuk*, fun. *Sanuk* refers to a sense of pleasure or happiness in either work or play. Buddhist religion teaches people to enjoy life the way it is. It tells people to be ready to have fun and enjoy themselves, because life is too short to take it too seriously. All things will pass. Nothing stays the same. Enjoy the here and now, and accept whatever the future will bring.

The national religion, Buddhism, teaches the Thai to believe only what they themselves realize as true, drawing on their own experience. The Lord Buddha told his disciples, "Do not believe me because I have told you this.

Believe me only if you have considered and found my words to be true." The Thai are taught to rely on themselves and their own inner wisdom. Every person is free to work in his own way to attain peace and happiness, according to his own ideas and his own capacity. One is free to choose one's own religion. According to the Thai constitution, the king must be Buddhist, but he supports all religions. In fact, the Thai Buddhist is taught to "Respect your friend's religions and parents as if they were your own. Do not belittle other people's beliefs or other people's elders."

Because the Thai Buddhist learns to accept life and the world the way they are, life is not seen in terms of a series of problems to be solved or evils to be exposed. There is no desire to change and improve the world. The Thai will rather accept what is, and are generally willing to incorporate new attitudes and new patterns of behavior into their lives. The Thai do not think it is necessary to strive mightily to make life good. It is good, if it is accepted.

The story is told of an American who saw a Thai man sitting in the shade of a tree just doing nothing. The American asked, "Dear Friend, how can you sit here doing nothing? Why don't you work?"

"Why should I work?" asked the Thai.

"Well, if you work hard you will earn a lot of money. If you work for many years, one day you will be rich. Then you will be free to do anything you want. You could travel, go where you want, or just sit and do nothing."

The Thai looked at the American incredulously. "But that is what I am doing now. Just sitting here, doing nothing."

The Thai have many reasons to smile. The word "thai" means "free" and the country, like its name, is free from western colonization. The Thai enjoy their freedom and their individualism. This attitude is well expressed in the folk saying "One who can do as one likes is a genuine Thai!"

Comparative Notes and Sources for Tales

Thai Folktale Genre

We arrived at our groupings for these tales only after studying the work of several Thai folktale scholars. The work of Kingkaew 'Atthakorn and Kulap Mullikamas as quoted in Preecha Vitragoon's work on the Thai folktale were especially helpful, as was *Phun Isan*, a publication of the Krom Sinlapakon in Bangkok. These are cited in our bibliography. Each person writing about the Thai folktale seems to use slightly different terms in discussing the tales. Of course, as in any body of folklore, a tale may fit into different genre depending on its use. Tales which attach themselves to one spot, becoming local legends or *tamnan*, for example, usually fit also into another genre. All of the genre names used here are in common usage in Thai culture, except for *Nithan Songkhruang*, which simply means "elaborate nithan." The term has been used by some Thai folklorists and there seems to be no more accurate term for the lengthy fairy tale which is so popular in Thai folk literature. We selected only two samples of this genre for inclusion here, though many volumes could be filled with the Thai treasure trove of these magical tales.

We placed only four of our tales in the *Nithan Chadok* (Jataka Tales) section. Though in the West we have learned to think of Jataka tales as stories taking place during the Buddha's rebirths, in Thai Buddhism the term *Chadok* has come to be associated with any story which explicates one of the canons of Buddhism. Over time the moral sayings which the Buddha's rebirth stories exemplified have acquired *other* stories to explicate them. But they are still called *Chadok*.

We include eight examples of *Nithan Son Khati Tam*, literally "Tales teaching you to think about Dharma." These moral tales are also known as *Nithan Ing Tamma* (Tales to lead you toward Dharma). These and the *Chadok* are well known in Thailand and are passed on by the monks through their teaching, as well as being used within the family to instill moral values in children.

Other genre selected for this collection are: *Nithan Gohok* (Tales of lying), *Nithan Talok* (Tales of humor), *Nithan Ruang Sat* (Tales of stories of animals), and *Thep Niyai* (Deity stories).

A Note on Motif and Type Numbers Used

The Stith Thompson *Motif-Index to Folk-Literature* provides a classification scheme for world folktales. Each part of a tale is given a distinct motif number. Thus "The Elephants and the Bees" could be classified both under A2335.3 *Origin and nature of animal's proboscis* and under B481.3 *Helpful bees*. World folktales are also classified according to a tale Type Index created by the Finnish folklorist Antti Aarne and updated in cooperation with Indiana University folklorist Stith Thompson. This is referred to here as the Aarne/Thompson Type Index. Each folktale is assigned only one type number. Not every folktale can be found in their Type Index, but most tales can be classified, at least in part, through the six-volume *Motif-Index*. The purpose of these strange looking numbers is to help you compare the tale you are reading with similar tales from around the globe, should you become interested in comparative folklore.

You will also find reference here to *The Storyteller's Sourcebook* by Margaret Read MacDonald. This work uses the Stith Thompson *Motif-Index* classification scheme to index over 550 folktale collections written for children.

Notes on Tale Sources

When referring to dates please note that B.E. means Buddhist Era. To calculate the A.D. date simply subtract 543 from the B.E. date.

"Lung Ta, the Calm Woodcutter." A fine version of this tale appears in *Nithan Phunmuang Khong Thai* by Yut Detkhamron (Bangkok: Khlangwitthaya, 2521 B.E., 6-8). It was collected from Chat Soichaturon, an official in the Department of Education at Chiangmai.

This tale has many variations in Thailand. The tall tale is often associated with United States folklore, but clearly tall tale telling has a strong tradition in Thailand as well. This tale could be classified as Stith Thompson Motif X980 *Lie: occupational or professional skill.*

"The Liar's Compete." A variant of this tale is found in *Nithan Thongthin Khong Thai* by Yut Detkhamron (Bangkok: Khlangwitthaya, 2531 B.E., 13-15). The story was collected from Phra Maha Udom Sangmani, a Buddhist monk in Trang.

This tale is a variant of Motif X909.4 *Second liar's tale must be accepted by first liar as it complements his own lie.* MacDonald's *Storyteller's Sourcebook* gives variants of this motif from China, England, Liberia (Vai), Portugal, Rumania, the United States, and Vietnam. The lying tale is popular throughout Thailand with many variations appearing. The notion of a liar's contest often figures in these tales.

"The Marvelous Canning Factory." Supaporn Vathanaprida heard this tale in her teen years in Lampang during the 1950s. Pineapple and sugar cane factories, an electrical plant, and a pottery factory brought surprising new technology to the town. Su feels this tall tale was a response to these technological implants into Thai culture. A version of this tall tale appears in *Nithan Phunmuang Khong Thai* by Yut Detkhamron (Bangkok: Khlang-witthaya, 2521 B.E., 26-27). His tale was collected from Thongchai Roi-kaenchan of Lampang.

This amazing tall tale seems to have no parallel in the Stith Thompson motif-index. It could be classed as X1030 *Lie: remarkable building*. The unusual reverse process motif is delightful.

"The Liar's Contest of the King." A well-told version of this story appears in *Nithan Phunmuang Khong Thai* by Yut Detkhamron (Bangkok: Khlangwit-thaya, 2521 B.E., 53-57). It was collected from Man Sisuwan, a Department of Education official in Pathumthani.

For a similar tale, see Stith Thompson Motif H342.1 *Suitor test: forcing princess to say "That's a lie."* Many European variants of the tale are given in the Stith Thompson *Motif-Index*, under Motif X905 *Lying contests*. MacDonald's *Storyteller's Sourcebook* cites several tales in which a liar tricks a judge into agreeing with a lie or incriminating himself. Tales from Burma, Russia, and West Africa are given. *The Types of the Folktale* lists several European variants of a similar tale under Type 1920C *The Master and the Peasant. The Master brought the peasant to say "You lie."* For an interesting Burmese liar's contest see "The Three Young Men Who Told Tall Stories" in *Burmese and Thai Fairy Tales* by Eleanor Brockett (Chicago: Follett, 1965, 79-83).

"Drinking with Yommaban, The King of the Dead." A delightful version of this was collected by Yut Detkhamron from Phra Winaikoson, a Bhuddhist monk at Wat Chediluang. The tale appears in *Nithan Phun-muang Khong Thai* by Yut Detkhamron (Bangkok: Khlangwitthaya, 2521 B.E., 313-315).

No variant of this tale appears in Stith Thompson's *Motif-Index*. It could be classified as K551.22.1 *A year's time granted to settle affairs before death*. Tales of tricking Death out of one's soul are common in European lore. See K210 *Devil cheated of his promised soul* for examples. This Thai tale, in which the King of the Dead becomes drunk and makes a mistake in his Book of Fate (N115) seems unique.

"Sri Thanonchai." Sri Thanonchai stories are known throughout Thailand, though in some areas he is known as Siengmieng. A seemingly endless string of humorous anecdotes have become attached to this trickster monk. Montri Umavijani includes an article "Sri Thanonchai Murals" in his *Facets of Thai Cultural Life* (Bangkok: Foreign News Division, Government Public Relations Department, Office of the Prime Minister, 1984, 54-60). He tells us that Sri Thanonchai's adventures date from the Ayutthaya period (1350-1767 A.D.). That article includes photos of murals depicting Sri Thanonchai tales, which adorn the walls of Wat Pathum Wanarum, a Bhuddist temple built in Bangkok by King Mongkut in 1857.

For more Sri Thanonchai anecdotes, see Umavijani's article, and "Siengmieng, the Minister" in *The Serpent Prince: Folktales from Northeastern Thailand* by Kermit Krueger (New York: World, 1969, 144-150).

For Lao variants, see "Xieng Mieng Stories" in *Encircled Kingdom: Legends and Folktales of Laos* by Jewell Reinhart Coburn. (Thousand Oaks, Calif.: Burn, Hart and Company, 1979, 37-40).

"Sri Thanonchai and the King." For another variant of this tale, see "Siengmieng, the Minister" in *The Serpent Prince* (New York: World, 1969, 144-150). Sri Thanonchai seems not to be the only monk to use this plot. Bankei was once challenged by an arrogant Nichiren priest who claimed Bankei could not *make* him obey. "Come up here and I will show you," said Bankei. "Come over to my left side." Bankei smiled. "No we may talk better if you are on my right side." The priest followed Bankei's directions. "You see, you *are* obeying me. I think you are a receptive person. Now sit down and listen." You will find a version of this anecdote in *Zen Flesh, Zen Bones: A Collection of Zen and Pre-Zen Writings* by Paul Rep (Garden City, N.Y.: Doubleday, 1961, 8-9).

"Sri Thanonchai and the Two Moons." The use of reflections is a common trick in world folklore. Stith Thompson lists several under J1791 *Reflection in water thought to be the original of the thing reflected*. Many tales are told of numbskulls who think the moon has fallen into the water and try to fish it out (J1791.2 *Rescuing the moon*.) K1715.1 *Weak animal shows strong his own reflection and frightens him* is another motif found worldwide, using a reflection to trick an adversary. This appears in the Indian *Panchatantra* and is told throughout Asia. However, the *two moon* variant is unusual. Score one for Sri Thanonchai.

"Sri Thanonchai's Special Dishes." This tale appears in *Ruam Nithan* by Phikkhu Pho Saenyanupap (Bangkok: Somchai Kanphim, 2528 B.E., 19-22). MacDonald's *Storyteller's Sourcebook* classifies this as H1304.2.1 *King* seeking wise man to appoint, asks to bring best dish in world. Applicant brings tongue. Tongue sings, gives orders, etc. Therefore is best. Asked to bring worst dish. Brings tongue. Variants are given from Cuba and from the African-American tradition in Alabama. Stith Thompson cites a Spanish example under H604 *Symbolic meaning of spiced and bitter tongue served at dinner.*

"Why the Bear Has a Short Tail." A variant of this tale appears in *Nithan Phunmuang Khong Thai* by Yut Detkhamron (Bangkok: Khlangwitthaya, 2521 B.E., 353-357). The tale was collected from Suan Ketima of Maesap School, Amphoe Samoeng, Chiangmai City.

This tale includes Motif A2478.4.2 *Why bear has short tail.* and K11.1 *Race won by deception: relative helpers.* The K11.1 motif is a common one throughout the world. MacDonald's *Storyteller's Sourcebook* cites variants from Brazil, Ceylon, East Africa, Germany, Haiti, India, Indonesia, Jamaica, Liberia (Mano), Poland, the United States (African-American, Cherokee, Iroquois, Seneca), the West Indies, and Zaire (Luban). Usually these tales involve a race on foot or in the air. The Thai adaptation of this theme to a vocal contest seems unusual. However a similar tale does appear in East Africa. Eleanor Heady's *Safiri the Singer* (27-30), describes a calling contest between the coucal bird and elephant. Each calls to his wife to prepare dinner. Coucal's soft call is passed on by other coucals and he wins.

"Tiger Seeks Wisdom." This tale may be found in *Nithan Phunban nai Changwat Surin-Srisaket*, compiled by Sun Watthanatham Changwat Surin, Witthayalai Khru Surin (Bangkok: 2527 B.E., 94-95), and in *Nithan Phunmuang Khong Thai* by Yut Detkhamron (Bangkok: Khlangwitthaya, 2521 B.E., 331-333). Collected from Prasert Muangín and Pasit Chommawan, Thamai Í School, Amphoe Muang, Chiangmai City.

This is Motif K341.8.1 *Trickster pretends to ride home for tools to perform tricks. Rides away on horse.* The motif is popular in European trickster tales. MacDonald's *Storyteller's Sourcebook* cites variants from Russia (Tatar), Scandinavia, Turkey, the United States (Native American), and Vietnam. Vietnamese versions in which a farmer tricks a tiger are found in *The Toad Is the Emperor's Uncle* by Vo-Dinh (Garden City, N.Y.: Doubleday, 1970, 65-73) and in *Vietnamese Legends* by George F. Schultz (Rutland, Vt.: Charles Tuttle, 1965,15-18).

In the version in *Nithan Phunban nai Changwat Surin-Srisaket*, a tiger is tricked by an elephant trainer when the tiger threatens to eat the man's elephant.

"The Elephants and the Bees." A good version of this tale is found in *Nithan Chaoban Khong Thai* by Yut Detkhamron (Bangkok: Khlangwitthaya, 2521 B.E., 470-472). The story was collected from Phloi Phattanrot of the Ministry of Education, Petchaboon City.

This seems a unique tale. It includes motifs A2335.3 *Origin and nature of animal's proboscis* and B481.3 *Helpful bees*. It might be fun to compare this story with Rudyard Kipling's tale of "How the Elephant Got His Trunk" in his *Just So Stories*.

"Power and Wisdom." This tale is well-known throughout Southeast Asia. A version of this tale appears in *Nithan Phunmuang Khong Thai* by Yut Detkhamron (Bangkok: Khlangwitthaya, 2521 B.E., 119-121). The story was collected from Ínchan Sombatnan, of the Ministry of Education, Amphoe Chomthong, Chiangmai.

Here is Stith Thompson Motif K1715.1 *Weak animal shows strong animal his own reflection and frightens him.* As one of the Jataka tales, this is well-known in India and Southeast Asia. MacDonald's *Storyteller's Sourcebook* cites variants from Afghanistan, Burma, China, India, Russia, and West Africa. Best known is the Indian Jataka variant (see chapter 4 for a discussion of the Jatakas); a classic retelling appears in Arthur Ryder's *The Panchatantra* (Chicago: University of Chicago, 1956, 81-88).

You might enjoy comparing the Thai and Indian variants with Hugh Sturton's Hausa tale in *Zomo the Rabbit* (New York: Atheneum, 1966, 26-38) and Mirra Ginsburg's Russian variant in *Three Rolls and One Doughnut* (New York: Dial, 1970, 45-46).

"The Deer Buddha." Variants of this tale, "Phya Kwang Phothisat", appear in *Niyai Íng Thamma* by Satra (pseud.) (Bangkok: Saemwitbannakhan, 2532 B.E., 1-10), and in *Nithan Chadok. Chut Satpa Himmaphan. Lem I* by Phaeng Onlao (Bangkok: LSE, 2434 B.C., 83-88). MacDonald's *Storyteller's Sourcebook* lists six Indian sources for this Jataka under B241.2.10 *The Banyan Deer*. For an extended ending to the story of the Banyan Deer see "The Banyan Deer" in *The Hungry Tigress: Buddhist Legends and Jataka Tales* by Rafe Martin (Berkeley, Calif.: Parallax Press, 1990, 90-97).

"Seven Stars." This tale appears in *Duai Panya Lae Khwamrak: Nithan Chao Muang Nua: Khon Muang, Lua, Thaiyai, Khoen, Lao* by Vagn Plenge (Bangkok: Siam Society and Samnakphin Samakhom Sangkhomsat Haeng Prathet Thai, 2529 B.E., 1-4) and in *Burmese and Thai Fairy Tales* by Eleanor Brockett (Chicago: Follett, 1965, 1-4).

Many tales in world folklore explain the origin of the Pleiades. A773 *Origin of Pleiades*. MacDonald's *Storyteller's Sourcebook* classified the Thai tale as A773.9 *Mother Hen killed as food for Phyain, Protector of the Buddha*, listing only the Brockett source given above. In this variant, the hen sacrifices herself for Phyain, the Protector of the Buddha.

"The Honest Woodcutter." This tale was heard by Supaporn Vathanaprida during her youth in Lampang. The tale is widely known throughout Asia and Europe. It appears as a fable of Aesop. The tale is Motif Q3.1 *Woodsman and the gold axe. A woodsman lets his axe fall into water. Hermes (or goddess) comes to his rescue. Takes out gold axe, but woodsman says that it is not his. Given his own axe and rewarded for his modest choice. His companion tries this plan and loses axe.*

A Japanese variant appears in Yoshiko Uchida's *The Magic Listening Cap* (New York: Harcourt, Brace, 1955, 73-81). For a Russian variant, see *Tales People Tell in Russia* by Lee Wyndham (New York: Messner, 1970, 43-46) or *13 Goblins* by Dorothy Gladys Spicer (New York: Coward-McCann, 1969, 28-34). Stith Thompson's *Motif-Index of Folk-Literature* lists Latvian and Chinese variants of this tale, and cites Lappish and Japanese variants under F420.5.1.7.4 *Water-sprite returns to the woodchopper a silver axe in place of the one he has lost.*

"The Thieving Crow." This story was well known to Supaporn Vathanaprida as a young girl growing up in Northern Thailand. The tale is a variant of Stith Thompson Motif K359.4 *Crow makes friends with pigeon so as to be able to steal food in household to which he belongs. Cook catches crow and pigeon must leave because of association.* For a Ceylonese variant, see *The Wonderful Wooden Peacock Flying Machine and Other Tales of Ceylon* by Ruth Tooze (New York: Day, 1969, 100-102). For a rendition of the Jataka from India see Joseph Jacobs, *Indian Folk and Fairy Tales* (New York: Putnam, n.d., 270-272) or Joseph Gaer, *Fables of India* (Boston: Little, Brown, 1955, 166-171).

This Thai variant differs from the others. It stresses the importance of gratitude and the evil of thievery. The variants cited above do not mention those topics, but dwell instead on the danger of bad associations.

"Who Is Best?" This tale was heard by Supaporn Vathanaprida from her maternal grandmother. Su believes her grandmother heard the tale from the monks at the monastery that she visited for an overnight meditative stay each month.

A variant of this story is also found in *Nithan Phunmuang Khong Thai* by Yut Detkhamron (Bangkok: Klangwitthaya, 2521 B.E., 294-296). It was collected from Mr. Bunyong Inthachak, a teacher in Mutkatawantok School, Amphoe Hot, Chiangmai.

This tale resembles Aarne/Thompson Type Index 841 *One Beggar Trusts God, the Other the King* and Stith Thompson Motif N351 *Money (Treasure) unwittingly given away*. The Aarne/Thompson Type Index cites Chinese, European, Indian, Japanese, and Turkish variants of this tale. You might also like to compare this tale to H621 *Skillful companions create a woman. To whom does she belong?* Both MacDonald's *Storyteller's Sourcebook* and Stith Thompson's *Motif-Index* cite several variants.

"The Pious Son-in-Law." This tale appears in *Ámata Nithan Thai* by Yut Detkahamron (Bangkok: Khlangwitthaya, 2521 B.E., 97-101). The story was collected from Phra Pricha Panyaphalo, a monk in Prajinburi City.

The tale reminds one of the Spanish/Islamic tale of the man who refuses to say "Inshallah" or "Si Dios Quiere" ("If God Wills It") (N385.1). The man is brought low and forced to admit that all happens only at God's pleasure. Still, in the Thai tale there is no divine hand at work, simply the normal scheme of things—nothing is certain, all things must pass.

"He Who Thinks He Is First Is Unwise." A variant of this tale may be found in *Nithan Thongthin Khong Thai* by Yut Detkhamron (Bangkok: Khlangwitthaya, 2531 B.E., 1-5). The story was collected from Kasem Sawasdi of Amphoe Maetaeng, Chiangmai.

This unusual tale of the search for a greater man begins much like the Stith Thompson Motif H1312 *Quest for the greatest of fools*, a popular European tale motif. But the tale soon becomes distinctly Thai in its tall tale imagery and its "pride brought low" (L400) moral. The Stith Thompson *Motif-Index* has no place to categorize the tall tale elements of this story, since tall tales are automatically considered humorous exaggeration in Western culture. In this Thai tale the far-fetched examples are *instructive* rather than humorous.

"Plenty." This tale is found in *Nithan Phunmuang Khong Thai* by Yut Detkhamron (Bangkok: Khlangwitthaya, 2521 B.E., 168-169). The story was collected from Yong Ínthachak of Mutkatawantok School in Amphae Hot, Chiangmai.

Under W251.2.1 *Greed*. MacDonald's *Storyteller's Sourcebook* lists several tales in which greed brings one low, but none quite like this. Under J514 *One should not be too greedy*, MacDonald cites a tale of Mother Luck, who fills a bag with gold until the man says "Enough." He never says "Enough" and the bag breaks. For this Latvian tale see Mae Durham's *Tit for Tat* (New York: Harcourt, Brace & World, 1967, 93-95).

"The Good Boy." This story is widely known in Supaporn Vathanaprida's home in Northern Thailand. A good version appears in *Nithan Phun-muang Khong Thai* by Yut Detkhamron (Bangkok: Khlangwitthaya, 2521 B.E., 132-135). The story was collected from Kaew Prasit of the Ministry of Education, Uthaithani.

This story reminds us of Motif B381 *Androcles and the Lion.* MacDonald's *Storyteller's Sourcebook* cites several Indian variants in which a thorn is pulled from an elephant's foot, earning undying gratitude for the hero. In this Thai tale the simple act of paying respect is enough to win the elephant's friendship for life. The image of the elephants responding to the sound of the bell is memorable. The tale includes Thompson Motifs D1213 *Magic bell* and B443.3 *Helpful elephant.*

The Buddha is said to have once stopped a raging elephant, standing gently in its path. See "Nalagiri the Elephant" in *The Hungry Tigress: Buddhist Legends & Jataka Tales* by Rafe Martin (Berkeley, Calif.: Parallax Press, 1990, 30-35).

"Medicine to Revive the Dead." This tale appears in *Ruam Nithan* by Phikkhu Phosaenyanuphap (Bangkok: Thammabucha, 1985, 119-126). This story also appeared in a sermon given by Phra Ratchananthamuni of Wat Chonprathanrangsarit, Amphoe Pakkret, Changwat Nonthaburi on Sunday, August 19, 2516 B.C. The sermon is reprinted in a memorial booklet for Sanga Pootrakul, *'Anuson Sanga Pootrakul* (Bangkok: Rongphim Ak-sonsamphan, 2521 B.C.).

This motif is similar to Stith Thompson N135.3 *The luck bringing shirt. The king is to become lucky when he puts on the shirt of a lucky man. The only man who says that he is lucky has no shirt.* (Type 844). Thompson also lists Motif H1394 *Quest for person who has not known sorrow,* but cites only European variants for both. MacDonald's *Storyteller's Sourcebook* mentions a Cambodian variant in which the cure for trouble is said to be a mustard seed from a home which has no troubles. To compare this tale with our Thai tale see *Trickster Tales* by I. G. Edmonds (Philadelphia: Lippincott, 1966, 86-90).

"When Death Comes." This tale is found in *Niyai Íng Thamma* by Satra (pseud.) (Bangkok: Soemwitbannakhan, 2532 B.E., 271-278). This story also appeared in a sermon given by Phra Ratchananthamuni of Wat Chonprathanrangsarit, Amphoe Pakkret, Changwat Nonthaburi on Sunday, August 19, 2516 B.C. The sermon is reprinted in a memorial booklet for Sanga Pootrakul, *'Anuson Sanga Pootrakul* (Bangkok: Rongphim Akson-samphan, 2521 B.C.).

The Stith Thompson *Motif-Index* seems to contain no entry for this motif. A487.0.1 *Death kills only those whose turn it is to die* misses the point of this tale...that death is irreversible and so grieving achieves nothing.

"If It Belongs To Us, It Will Come To Us." A variant of this tale appears in *Nithan Phunmuang Khong Thai* by Yut Detkhamron (Bangkok: Khlangwitthaya, 2521 B.E., 195-196). The story was collected from Riap Rainakon of Amphoe Phrao, Chiangmai.

Variants of this motif are widely distributed throughout the world. MacDonald's *Storyteller's Sourcebook* lists variants from Afghanistan, Brazil, Japan, Mexico, North Africa and Vietnam. See N182.1 *Man dreams gold falls on head, refuses discovered pot of gold in garden. Greedy neighbor digs it up and finds it full of snakes* and following motifs.

The Thai variant, with its emphasis on the inevitability of life, suggests comparison of this tale with Stith Thompson's N141 *Luck or intelligence? Dispute as to which is more powerful. Man with intelligence remains poor (is brought into court). Saved by mere luck.* MacDonald's *Storyteller's Sourcebook* lists variants of this motif from Czechoslovakia, Denmark, Greece, Latvia, North Africa, Poland, Portugal, and Romania, and there are Jewish variants.

Note that the Western tale attributes good fortune to luck, a concept not identical to the Thai concept of inevitability. Most variants of the good neighbor-bad neighbor tale stress only the suitable reward motif: good receives good, bad receives bad. It is only in the Thai version that the story is made to carry a more obvious moral.

"Muang Laplae." This story appears in many Thai folktale collections. It can be found in *Nithan Phunban Thai* by Wisan Banthawong (Bangkok: Soemwitbannakhan, 2523 B.E., 207-216) and in *Nithan Phunban Khong Thongthin Sukhothai lae Boriwen Doi Rop* Phitsanulok, Sun Sukhothai Suksa, Mahawitthayalai Srinakharinwirot University, 2522 B.E., 48).

This tale resembles F302.4.2 *Fairy comes into man's power when he steals her wings (clothes).* In this case her leaf is stolen. In many European and Asian tales the man keeps the fairy's garment/wings/skin and she is forced to live with him until, by accident, she finds her garment and leaves. The man here returns her object at once and is taken to fairyland to live with her (F302.1 *Man goes to fairyland and marries fairy*). He must leave, however, when he breaks a fairyland taboo (F378.0.1), a common motif in folktales. The fairy gold (F342.1) is also a common folktale device. It appears to be worthless dross and is tossed aside, only to have its true value discovered too late.

"Mouse Island and Cat Island." This tale is found in *Nithan Phunban Thai* by
Wisan Banthawong. (Bangkok: Soemwitbannakhan, 2532 B.E., 342-344).
Khrut is a popular mythological figure in Thai folk literature. He is
sometimes helpful, sometimes sassy and dangerous. Khrut is the Garuda
of Indian mythology where he is the transport of Vishnu. In Indian
tradition, he roams the world devouring evil men.

The second half of this tale uses Motif D882.1 *Stolen object stolen back by
helpful cat and dog.* Also Type 560 *The Magic ring. The grateful animals (cat and
dog) recover it for him.* Both MacDonald and Stith Thompson cite many variants
for this tale, from throughout the world. However this Thai variant is unusual
in that the animals confront the mouse, rather than stealing the object back.
And, of course, the localized ending, in which the main characters all become
landmarks, is distinct to this tale.

"Kaeo, the Horse-Face Girl." Variants of this tale can be found in *Nithan
Phunban Thai: Kaeo Nama* by Phon Khachonsak (Bangkok: Samnakphim
Deknoi, 2533 B.E.) and *Phun Isan: Tamnan Lae Nithan Phunban Isan* by
Krom Sinlapakon. Kong Borankhadi [Fine Arts Dept., Archeology Divi-
sion]. Bangkok: Krom Sinlapakon, 2531 B.E., 44+).

This is an elaborate tale of epic proportions. The opening scene, in which
Kaeo confiscates the prince's fallen kite, reminds us of certain variants of
Aarne/Thompson Type 402 *The Mouse (Cat, Frog, etc.) as Bride.* In some
versions of that tale, the prince shoots an arrow and follows where it falls to
meet an ungainly bride-to-be, often a frog. One thinks also of *The Frog Prince*
(Type 440) who takes possession of the fallen ball of the princess.

The king sends Kaeo on a quest to earn the prince, another familiar
western motif. A hermit helps her with a magic knife and flying machine. The
prince has gone off to marry someone else and Kaeo follows, turns herself into
a beauty, and wins his love. But here, the story takes a decidedly Asian turn.
Her husband is kidnapped by giants, so Kaeo disguises herself as a man and
slays the giant's king to rescue him. (K2357.6 *Woman disguises as man to enter
enemy's camp. Slays enemy king.*) Then she (as a man) and her husband defeat
the remainder of the giants and restore the kingdom to its rightful rulers. They
are given the hands of two maids in reward, but Kaeo passes on this and lets
husband Prince Pinthong take both girls. But there are still more giants to slay
and the very pregnant Kaeo meets Prakaikrot on the battlefield, slaying him,
then giving birth to triplets! The three young princesses are kidnapped by a
giant eagle, rescued and reared by a hermit, and wooed by three princes, who
must fight them for their hands. Being equally matched, their wedding is
allowed. Lastly, their brother comes to rescue the princesses, finds them
happily married and restores them to their family. An elaborate and incredible
tale, most notable for its amazing women warriors. Though western folklore

shows women disguising as men for trickery, they seldom go headlong into battle. Stith Thompson's K2357.6 *Woman disguises as man to enter enemy's camp. Slays enemy king* cites only one variant, an Italian tale.

"Chet Huat Chet Hai." This tale may be found in *Nithan Phunban nai Changwat Surin-Srisaket*, compiled by Sun Wathanatham Changwat Surin, Witthay-alai Khru Surin, (Cultural Center of Surin City, Surin Teachers College, 2527, 116-131), in *Phun Isan: Tamnan Lae Nithan Phunban Isan* by Kong Borankhadi, Krom Sinlapakon (Bangkok: Krom Sinlapakon, 2531 B.E., 52-57), in *Duai Panya Lae Khwamrak: Nithan Chao Muangnua: Khon Muang, Lua, Thaiyai, Khoen, Lao* compiled by Vagn Plenge (Bangkok: Siam Society and Samnakphim Samakhom Sangkhomsat Haeng Prathet Thai, 2519 B.E., 46), and in *Wannakam Phunban Chak Tambon Rungkayai, Amphoe Phimai, Changwat Nakhon Ratchasima* by Preecha Vitragoon (Bangkok: Nuai Suksa Nithet Kromkan Fukhat Khru, 2521 B.E., 136-142). The tale is also found in *Watthanatham Lanna Thai* by Manee Phayomyong. (Bangkok: Thai Watthanapanick, 2529 B.C., 240-243), and in *Khati Chaoban Isan* by Charuwan Thammawat (Bangkok: Ákson Watthama, 1978).

Tales of abandoned children are common in folklore. Stith Thompson's *Motif-Index* includes six pages of citations for S300-S399 *Abandoned or murdered children*. S321 *Destitute parents abandon children* cites tales from China, India, and Korea. The abandonment theme is familiar in Western tales such as "Hansel and Gretel" and "Babes in a Wood." F612.1 *Strong hero sent from home because of enormous appetite* is also a motif found elsewhere in the world. Stith Thompson cites variants from Brittany, Indonesia, Norway, and the Philippines. And F615 *Strong man evades death. Vain attempts to kill him* has variants from Ireland, India, the Philippines, and the United States (Native American). Still none of these put the tale ingredients together in quite the same way as this distinctive Thai tale. In the end, Chet Huat Chet Hai meets up with remarkable companions F601 *Extraordinary companions. A group of men with extraordinary powers travel together* and together they conquer a witch. For a Burmese variant of this tale see "The Diminutive Flute Player" in *The Oryx Multicultural Folktale Series: Tom Thumb* by Margaret Read MacDonald (Phoenix: Oryx, 1993, 85-87). This tale, taken from a version by Maung Htin Aung, lacks the extrordinary companions motif.

"Twin Stars." This tale is known throughout Thailand. A variant is found in *Nithan Thongthin Khong Thai* by Yut Detkhamron. (Bangkok: Khlang-withaya, 2521 B.E., 390). The story was collected from Phong Chuanpra-soet, Ban Huainamrin, Amphoe Maerim, Chiangmai.

MacDonald's *Storyteller's Sourcebook* classifies this tale under A778 *Origin of the Milky Way*. This is a popular Asian tale, often repeated on the occasion of the seventh night of the seventh moon. In several Asian countries the seventh night of the seventh moon is a festival occasion. This festival seems not to have caught on in Thailand, though the story is told. For variants of this tale from China, Japan, and Vietnam, see *The Storyteller's Sourcebook*. Usually the tale is told of a spinning maid and a cowherd. They are set in the sky on opposite sides of the Milky Way. Magpies (or ravens) form a bridge once a year for the lovers to cross. Their tears of joy in meeting and tears of sorrow at parting fall as rain on that night. The Japanese festival of Tanabata celebrates the meeting of these lovers. Romantic poems are written to the memory of their love and hung decoratively on bamboo stalks in the yard or home. The next day, they may be thrown into a stream to be carried away by the current.

The Chinese celebrate this day as Chhit Sek (Chilsuk), the Double Seventh. Trays are offered on this night to the Seven Sisters, one of whom became the cowherd's lover. For accounts of celebration of the Seventh Day of the Seventh Moon in China, Japan, Korea, and Taiwan, see *The Folklore of World Holidays* by Margaret Read MacDonald (Detroit: Gale Research, 1991, 384-388).

"Songkran: The Thai New Year's Story." This story is known by everyone in Thailand. Su learned the story as a child and continues to hear it annually when she attends Songkran services at the Thai Buddhist temple in Seattle. Printed versions may be found in *Khrongsang Sangkhom Lae Watthanatham Thai* by Ratchanikon Settho (Bangkok: Thai Watthanaphanit, 1989, 176-178) and in *Watthanatham Lanna Thai* by Manee Phayomyong (Bangkok: Thai Watthanapanit, 2529 B.E., 249-254).

This story includes Stith Thompson Motif B216 *Knowledge of animal languages*. In many cultures, we find tales of a hero whose kindness to animals is rewarded with knowledge of their speech. Later, he overhears information which saves him or brings him wealth. See MacDonald's *Storyteller's Sourcebook* for 23 variants of this theme from Africa (Nuer), Albania, Germany, Ghana (Akan), India, Nigeria (Yoruba), North Africa, Peru (Inca), Russia, Scotland, Switzerland, Vietnam, Wales, and Yugoslavia. This tale might also be said to include Stith Thompson Motif H543 *Escape from devil by answering the riddle*.

More Books to Read About Thailand

Thai Folktales

Brockett, Eleanor. *Burmese and Thai Fairy Tales*. Chicago: Follett, 1965.

Davies, Marian. *Tales from Thailand*. Rutland, Vt.: Charles E. Tuttle, 1971. Illustrated by Supee Pasutanavin.

Krueger, Kermit. *The Serpent Prince: Folktales from Northeastern Thailand*. New York: World, 1969. Illustrated by Yoko Mitsuhashi.

Buddhist Tales and Books About Buddhism

Edmonds, I. G. *Buddhism: A First Book*. New York: Franklin Watts, 1978.

Hodges, Margaret. *The Golden Deer*. New York: Charles Scribner's Sons, 1992. A picture book of this Jataka. Illustrated by Daniel San Souci.

Martin, Rafe. *The Hungry Tigress: Buddhist Legends and Jataka Tales*. Berkeley, Calif.: Parallax Press, 1990. An adult collection of Buddhist tales with commentary.

About Thailand

Harrison, Supenn, and Judy Monroe. *Cooking the Thai Way*. Minneapolis, Minn.: Lerner Publications, 1986. Easy-to-follow recipes. Photographs by Robert L. Wolfe and Diane Wolfe.

Goodman, Jim. *Cultures of the World: Thailand*. New York: Marshall Cavendish, 1991.

Schwabach, Karen. *Thailand: Land of Smiles*. Minneapolis, Minn.: Dillon Press, 1991.

Thomson, Ruth, and Neil Thomson. *A Family in Thailand*. Minneapolis, Minn.: Lerner, 1988, c.1987.

Fiction Set in Thailand

Ho, Minfong. *Rice Without Rain*. New York: Lothrop, Lee & Shepard, 1990. Ming is in love with a young rebel who wants her to flee with him and join the guerillas in the mountains. But her family and land call for her to stay. A young adult novel.

Ho, Mingfong. *Sing to the Dawn*. New York: Lothrop, Lee & Shepard, 1975. Dawon wants to attend high school in the city, but her father will allow only her brother to go for higher education. A juvenile novel.

Picture Books

Ayer, Jacqueline. *Nu Dang and His Kite*. New York: Harcourt, Brace, 1959. Dated in that it refers to Thailand as "Siam."

Ayer, Jacqueline. *The Paper-Flower Tree: A Tale from Thailand*. New York: Harcourt, Brace & Work, 1962. A young girl plants a paper flower, hoping a paper-flower tree will grow. Through the good graces of a passing peddlar, it does!

Ayer, Jacqueline. *A Wish for Little Sister*. New York: Harcourt, Brace, 1960. Dated in that it refers to Thailand as "Siam."

Meeker, Clare. *A Tale of Two Rice Birds*. Illustrated by Christine Lamb. Seattle, Wash.: Sasquatch Books, 1994.

Works Consulted

(B.E. = Buddhist era. To calculate the A.O. date subtract 543 from the B.E. date.)

Aarne, Antti, and Stith Thompson. *The Types of the Folktale*. Helsinki: Suomalainen Tiedeakatemia, 1973.

'Anuson Janpá Poutrakul. Bangkok: Rongphim 'Aksonjamphan, 2521 B.E.

Banthawong, Wisan. *Nithan Phunban Thai*. Bangkok: Soemwitbannakhan, 2523 B.E.

Brockett, Eleanor. *Burmese and Thai Fairy Tales*. Illustrated by Harry and Ilse Toothill. New York: Follett, 1965.

Coburn, Jewell Reinhart. *Encircled Kingdom: Legends and Folktales of Laos*. Thousand Oaks, Calif.: Burn, Hart and Company, 1979.

Detkhamron, Yut. *Ámata Nithan Thai*. Bangkok: Khlangwitthaya, 2521 B.E.

———. *Nithan Chaoban Khong Thai*. Bangkok: Khlangwithaya, 2521 B.E.

———. *Nithan Phunmuang Khong Thai*. Bangkok: Khlangwitthaya, 2521 B.E.

———. *Nithan Thai Saen Sanuk*. Bangkok: Khlangwitthaya, 2520 B.E.

———. *Nithan Thongthin Khong Thai*. Bangkok: Khlangwitthaya, 2521 B.E.

Khachonsak, Phon. *Nithan Phunban Thai: Kaeo Nama*. Illustrated by Bandek. Bangkok: Samnakphim Deknoi, 2533 B.E.

Krom Sinlapakon. Kong Borankhadi. (Department of Fine Arts. Archeological Division.) *Phun Isan: Tamnan Lae Nithan Phunban Isan*. Bangkok: Krom Sinlapakon, 2531 B.E.

Krueger, Kermit. *The Serpent Prince: Folk Tales from Northeastern Thailand*. Illustrated by Yoko Mitsuhashi. New York: World, 1969.

Loetphiriyakamon, Phairot. *Khati Chaoban Lanna Thai*. Chiangmai: Surivong Book Center, 2516 B.E.

MacDonald, Margaret Read. *The Folklore of World Holidays*. Detroit: Gale Research, 1991.

———. *The Oryx Multicultural Folktale Series: Tom Thumb*. Phoenix: Oryx, 1993.

———. *The Storyteller's Sourcebook: A Subject, Title, and Motif Index to Folklore Collections for Children*. Detroit: Neal-Schuman/Gale Research, 1982.

Martin, Rafe. *The Hungry Tigress: Buddhist Legends and Jataka Tales*. Berkeley, Calif: Parallax Press, 1990.

Nithan Phunban nai Changwat Surin-Srisaket. Compiled by Sun Wathanatham Changwat Surin and Witthayalai Khru Surin (Cultural Center of Surin City, Surin Teacher's College), 2527 B.E.

Onlao, Phaeng. *Nithan Chadok. Chut Satpa Himmaphan. Lem I*. Bangkok: LSE, 2434 B.E.

Phamnarong, Nakhorn. *Nithan Phunban Khong Thongthin Sukhothai lae Boriwen Doi Rop* Phitsanulok: Sun Sukhothai Suksa, Srinakharinwirot University, 2522 B.E.

Phayomyong, Manee. *Watthanatham Lanna Thai*. Bangkok: Thai Watthana-panit, 2529 B.E.

Phosaenyanuphap, Phikkhu. *Ruam Nithan*. Bangkok: Samnak Nangsu Tham-mabucha, 1985.

Plenge, Vagn. *Duai Panya Lae Khwam Rak: Nithan Chao Muang Nua: Khon Muang, Lua, Thaiyai, Khoen, Lao*. Bangkok: Siam Society and Samnakphim Samakhom Sangkhomsat Haeng Prathet Thai, 2519 B.E.

Ratchananthamuni, Phra. "Pathakatha Tham Khrangthi 6" in *'Anuson Sanga Pootrakul*. Sunday, August 19, 2516. Bangkok: Rongphim Áksonsamphan, 2521 B.E.

Satra. *Niyai Íng Thamma*. Bangkok: Saemwitbannakhan, 2532 B.E.

Settho, Ratchanikon. *Khrongsang Sangkhom Lae Watthanatham Thai*. Bangkok: Thai Watthanaphanit, 1989.

Sonthirak, Plaek. *Nithan Thai Chutthi 3. Chabab Nakrian*. Bangkok: Samnakphim Bannakit, 2522 B.E.

Thammmawat, Charuwan. *Khati Chaoban Isan*. Bangkok: Ákson Watthana, 1978.

Thompson, Stith. *Motif-Index of Folk-Literature*. Bloomington: Indiana University Press, 1954.

Toth, Marian Davies. *Tales from Thailand*. illus. by Supee Pasutanavin. Rutland, Vt.: Charles E. Tuttle, 1971.

Umavijani, Montri. *Facets of Thai Cultural Life*. Bangkok: Foreign News Division, Government Public Relations Department, Office of the Prime Minister, 1984.

Vitragoon, Preecha. *Wannakam Phunban Chak Tambon Rungkayai, Amphoe Phimai, Changwat Nakhon Ratchasima*. Bangkok: Nuai Suksa Nithet Kromkan Fukhat Khru, 2521 B.E.

บรรณานุกรมหนังสือ

Thai Language Works Consulted

บัณฑะวงศ์, วิสันต์. นิทานพื้นบ้านไทย ... กรุงเทพฯ : เสริมวิทย์บรรณาคาร, 2523.

เดชคำรณ, ยุทธ. อมตะนิทานไทย. กรุงเทพฯ : คลังวิทยา, 2521.

เดชคำรณ, ยุทธ. นิทานชาวบ้านของไทย. กรุงเทพฯ : คลังวิทยา, 2521.

เดชคำรณ, ยุทธ. นิทานพื้นเมืองของไทย. กรุงเทพฯ : คลังวิทยา, 2521.

เดชคำรณ, ยุทธ. นิทานไทยแสนสนุก. กรุงเทพฯ : คลังวิทยา, 2520.

เดชคำรณ, ยุทธ. นิทานท้องถิ่นของไทย. กรุงเทพฯ : คลังวิทยา, 2521.

ขจรศักดิ์, ภร. นิทานพื้นบ้านไทย: แก้วหน้าม้า. บ้านเด็ก เขียนภาพ. กรุงเทพฯ :
สำนักพิมพ์เด็กน้อย, 2533.

เลิศพิริยกมล, ไพรถ. คติชาวบ้าน ลานนาไทย. เชียงใหม่ : สุริวงศ์บุ๊คเซ็นเตอร์, 2516.

นิทานพื้นบ้านในจังหวัดสุรินทร์–ศรีสะเกษ. รวบรวมโดยศูนย์วัฒนธรรมจังหวัดสุรินทร์, 2527.

อ่อนละออ, แพง. นิทานชาดก ชุด สัตว์ป่าหิมพานต์. กรุงเทพฯ : ชมรมนักเรียนเก่า LSE
จัดพิมพ์, 2534.

พันธุ์ฌรงค์, นคร. นิทานพื้นบ้านของท้องถิ่นสุโขทัยและบริเวณโดยรอบ. พิษณุโลก : ศูนย์
สุโขไทยศึกษา มหาวิทยาลัยศรีนครินทรวิโรฒ, 2522.

พยอมยงค์, มณี. วัฒนธรรมล้านนาไทย. กรุงเทพฯ : ไทยวัฒนาพานิช, 2529.

โพธิ์แสนยานุภาพ, ภิกษุ. รวมนิทาน. กรุงเทพฯ : สำนักหนังสือธรรมบูชาของคณะ
เผยแพร่วิธีการดำเนินชีวิตอันประเสริฐ, 2528.

เพลงเออ, เวาน์. ด้วยปัญญาและความรัก นิทานชาวเมืองเหนือ คนเมือง ลื้อ ไทยใหญ่ เงิน
เล่า. เวาน์ เพลงเออ รวบรวม จรัญ อุปรานุเคราะห์ ช่วยเหลือ. สยามสมาคมและ
สำนักพิมพ์สมาคมสังคมศาสตร์แห่งประเทศไทย, 2519.

ราชนันทมุนี, พระ. "ปาฐกถาธรรมครั้งที่ 6" ใน อนุสรณ์ส่ง่า ภู่ตระกูล. วันอาทิตย์ ที่ 19
สิงหาคม 2516. กรุงเทพฯ : โรงพิมพ์อักษรสัมพันธ์, 2521.

สาตรา. นิยายอิงธรรมะ. กรุงเทพฯ : เสริมวิทย์บรรณาคาร, 2532.

เสฐโฐ, รัชนีกร. โครงสร้างสังคมและวัฒนธรรมไทย. กรุงเทพฯ : ไทยวัฒนาพานิช,
2532.

กรมศิลปากร. กองโบราณคดี. พื้นอีสาน : ตำนานและนิทานพื้นบ้านอีสาน. กรุงเทพฯ :
       กรมศิลปากร, 2531.
สนธิรักษ์, แปลก. นิทานไทย ชุดที่ 3 ฉบับนักเรียน. กรุงเทพฯ : สำนักพิมพ์บรรณกิจ,
       2522.
ธรรมวัตร, จารุวรรณ. คติชาวบ้านอีสาน ... กรุงเทพฯ : อักษรวัฒนา, 1978.
อุบตระกูล, ปรีชา. วรรณกรรมพื้นบ้านจากตำบลรังกาใหญ่ อำเภอพิมาย จังหวัดนครราชสีมา.
       เอกสารนิเทศการศึกษา ฉบับที่ 203 หน่วยศึกษานิเทศน์ กรมการฝึกหัดครู, 2521.

Index

About the Author and Editor

Supaporn Vathanaprida (on the right) received her MLS from the University of Washington and has worked with the King County Library System since 1969. Before coming to the United States, Su was a high school teacher in her hometown of Lampang, a city in Northern Thailand.

Since living in the United States, Su has become aware of the importance of preserving her own cultural roots. She has tried to pass along some of the Thai cultural heritage to her two daughters by training them in Thai classical music and dance. The two girls, along with Su's husband Chare, perform with the classical group *Siam Sangkit*.

The preparation of *Thai Tales* is yet another way in which Su hopes to share her Thai heritage.

Margaret Read MacDonald (on the left) has been a children's librarian at the Bothell Branch of the King County Library System since 1979. MacDonald earned her Ph.D. in Folklore from Indiana University and is known for her "tellable" folktale collections. She has written over a dozen books including *Twenty Tellable Tales, Look Back and See: 20 Lively Tales for Gentle Tellers,* and *Peace Tales: World Folktales to Talk About.* In editing this collection MacDonald broke with her usual style and tried to keep the language as close to Su Vathanaprida's texts as possible. MacDonald and Vathanaprida are now at work on several picture books based on Thai folktales.